Life is a Brief Opportunity for Joy

LIFE IS A BRIEF OPPORTUNITY FOR JOY

WILL MEYERHOFER

Mill City Press
Minneapolis, MN

Mill City Press, Inc.
212 3rd Avenue North, Suite 290
Minneapolis, MN 55401
612.455.2294
www.millcitypublishing.com

ISBN-13: 978-1-937600-47-1
LCCN: 2010940221

Cover Design by Christine Sullivan
Typeset by Sophie Chi

Printed in the United States of America

DEDICATION

For William Yan To Kwok,
my partner as we make our way forward,
hand in hand.

PREFACE

This book is a guide to discovering joy, the simple pleasure of living each day.

I am a psychotherapist, with an office in New York City. As I work with patients and listen to their stories, I search for themes that define the human condition.

These themes have melded into a philosophy centered upon living with joy.

No book can substitute for the process of psychotherapy.

But I hope these ideas will introduce you to the work of self-discovery at the heart of that experience.

There are a lot of ideas in this short book.

It might take some re-reading to digest them completely.

My sources are numerous and varied. I've drawn on the work of psychoanalysts I admire - people like Theodor Reik, Hyman Spotnitz, Louis Ormont, Fritz Perls and, of course, Sigmund Freud. There is a bit of neuroscience and evolutionary psychology, too, and smatterings of philosophy, literature, poetry and Buddhism.

Some ideas and much of the synthesis are original, inspired by my work with patients.

I encourage you to take a break from reading from time to time, and let your mind drift off into your own thoughts.

I have organized this book into two parts.

Part One focuses on becoming more conscious, and the process of discovering your best self, so you can take the role of the actor in your life instead of the audience.

Part Two explores the three elements of every life - playing, working and loving. Mastering these challenges brings joy to the life you lead.

This book and my work as a psychotherapist are about love. I care deeply about my patients and the work we do together.

I aspire to be your companion in a conversation and on a journey.

I hope you will pick up this book and learn a bit about joyful living, then perhaps share it with a friend, and pass on this gift.

PART ONE

CONSCIOUS LIVING

CHAPTER 1

Become Your Best Self

A lot of people don't like themselves.

As a therapist, I ask that question a lot - do you like who you are? It grieves me to hear the same answers over and over:

I don't like who I am.

There's something wrong with me.

I feel like a fake.

I can't do anything right.

I'm a loser.

On and on.

I like people. I try to see what's best in them. Most of the time, when I don't click with somebody or I find them hard to be with, it's because they don't really know themselves. They are unaware of the feelings bombarding them, the patterns they are unknowingly playing out.

There is a French saying: Tout comprendre, tout pardonner.

To understand completely is to forgive completely.

Becoming conscious of who you are - your authentic, best self – and how you think and feel, permits you to follow this prescription.

1

First you understand yourself.

Then you forgive yourself.

Then you can move on to love and care for yourself and others.

Do you like yourself?

If you know your best self, then the answer has to be yes, because you are in control of that identity. That's the person you want to be, the person you are starting to be right now.

The problem with unconscious living is that you aren't there, you're on auto-pilot. You might not like the person who takes over, but you can't rein him in, since you disappear when he shows up.

I blanked out.

I don't know what got into me.

Behind these excuses lies the fact that you ceded control. You were no longer the actor in your life, but a member of the audience.

Awareness brings out the best self. You show who you truly are when you start making the decisions, wide awake and in control.

Be your best self, right now. A lot of things will change.

As they say in twelve-step: It isn't easy, but it's simple.

Patients tell me it's too late for them. I tell them they're right – we'll wait until next year, when you're younger.

The time is now. You can change.

Awake to conscious living. Stop shutting down or avoiding or wearing a mask. Exist in the moment. Your best self is you.

Charles Dickens summarized the process of psychotherapy – oddly enough - in A Christmas Carol.

Whether you read the book, saw the Scrooged version with Bill Murray or the Disney version with Scrooge McDuck, it's all the same story.

Scrooge hoards money, yells at people who work for him and is generally an unpleasant person.

Christmas Eve brings ghosts representing his past, present and future, who visit Scrooge and review the events of his life.

He has an "ah-ha moment."

The next morning he races to show the world his best self, wishing everyone a Merry Christmas and buying a turkey for Tiny Tim.

He seems like a new guy – but in fact, that's the real Scrooge.

He was made aware of himself.

Awareness creates change.

That's the process of psychotherapy.

When you check out and become unconscious, unexamined feelings take over. These are emotions you don't wish to acknowledge, feel you shouldn't have or don't know are there.

You can act-out or act-in on these feelings.

Acting-out means going into action:

Smashing your fist on the table.

Acting-in means shutting down:

Refusing to answer the phone.

In some families, children learn to act-out. Their parents model it for them, and they imitate - yelling, slamming doors and breaking things.

Other kids learn to act-in - ignoring their schoolwork, hiding in their bedrooms.

These lessons stay with you.

If you are acting on an unconscious emotion, chances are you're angry.

Anger is the oldest, most primitive emotion.

Sometimes you don't want to be angry. You just are.

You can care very deeply for someone, and still be angry at him.

You might not even know why.

Anger is not rational and it doesn't need a reason. It just is.

Sometimes you want to put on dark glasses and a black leather jacket.

Get on a motorcycle.Be the tough guy.

It is tempting. Seems like fun.

It's just anger.

Discharging unconscious anger feels good.

That's why we live in a violent world.

We are not accustomed to admitting that discharging anger is gratifying.

It makes people nervous.

But it also makes good Darwinian, evolutionary sense that releasing aggression would feel good, since animals who enjoy fighting off predators survive to pass on their genes. It's the same principle that explains why sex feels good.

According to the Pleasure Principle, when you act unconsciously, you naturally seek gratification. The unconscious is basically a child – the child you were, who lives on within you. If he sees a shiny cupcake, he wants to eat that cupcake. He's not stopping to count calories. He wants something that feels good.

That's why the Pleasure Principle is a fundamental law of human psychology.

And that's why discharging anger - acting-out or acting-in – is often done unconsciously.

Some part of you is savoring a forbidden pleasure.

As a human, you contain an ancient indicator of unconscious gratification.

The corners of your mouth turn up.

Like your ape cousins, you display this behavior when you feel pleasure - when something bad happens to someone else.

You are sincerely concerned. But that hint of a smile says you're hiding a secret.

You don't want to admit it, but it feels good.

The Germans coined the word "schadenfreude" to describe how good it feels when something bad happens to someone you don't like. It is usually treated like a joke, something half-serious. But Schadenfreude is real.

You do enjoy the suffering of an enemy when you're angry.

In Schadenfreude, the implication is that you didn't seek the revenge yourself.

If you had, the laughing would stop.

We'd be witnessing something primitive, sadistic and human.

Murder. Torture. War.

You look for excuses to discharge anger.

Couples arrange catastrophic late night battles.

There might be a hangover in the morning, but it feels good now.

So you keep going.

If you can't discharge violence yourself, savor the violence of others.

The average eighteen-year-old has viewed two hundred thousand acts of violence on television.

Humans delight in reverting into beasts.

You are recently evolved from an ape.

You try to bury your primitive past.

Distance yourself from the animal within.

But if you bury anger, it reappears.

You round a street corner, and imagine confronting a mugger.

Kicking him to the ground.

You unload a torrent of abuse at a subway booth attendant.

Displaced anger.

It finds outlet in fleeting fantasies.

Or spontaneous melt-downs.

Ask yourself if you are angry right now.

Probably not. You have no reason to be.

But you are - not just because I'm telling you how you're feeling.

Although that makes you angry, too.

Most anger feels unjustified.

You're afraid you'll go into action if you own it, so you tuck it away.

But there is what you feel.

And there is how you act on those feelings.

Two different things.

To be your best self, you must know what you're feeling.

Put anger into words.

The monkeys at the zoo kiss and bite and chase and cuddle and play and screech and argue - all the things you do, except think.

That's where you have the upper hand.

The trick is to think like a human while feeling like a monkey.

If you only think and don't feel, your emotions will surface in unconscious acts.

But if you apply thought to your feelings, you will gain awareness to live as your best self.

Freud termed the conscious self a battlefield.

It can feel that way.

But if you understand your primitive, conflicting feelings, you can harness their energy to accomplish good.

That's what Martin Luther King did. He hated the oppression and injustice of the Jim Crow South. It made him angry.

King might have gone into action on his anger, resorting to violence.

Or acted in, shutting himself off from the world.

But King studied his feelings. He put them into words that moved mountains.

Brought us his best self and changed history.

Anger does not equal rage.

Rage is frustrated, impotent anger.

Anger with a purpose can inspire.

Don't fear anger – it coexists with love.

Own it. Experience your authentic self.

Buddhism is an early source of thinking about ourselves and the lives we lead. There is no denying the strong parallels between Buddhist thought and psychoanalysis.

No one knows the earliest source of psychoanalytic thought.

Freud founded the modern movement, but his inspiration dates much further back, to that first someone who pondered the day he was living.

The days he had lived.

And the days he had ahead of him.

And tried to make sense of it all.

I am not asking you to bow down before a statue of a fat, smiling guy and burn incense if you don't want to.

The Buddha's ideas are enough to fascinate and amaze.

When I speak of Buddhism, I do not refer to a religion, per se, but a collection of stories and philosophical writings attributed to the historic Buddha, Siddhartha Gautama, and his followers.

Siddhartha was an Indian prince who lived around 400 B.C.E.

As in ancient Greece, the existence of a pantheon of gods - many of the same deities that live on in modern Hinduism - was taken for granted.

But the Buddha never considered himself a god.

A famous story relates how the Buddha began to discover his best self.

His father, a local king, was fearful of a prophecy that his son, the prince, would become an ascetic.

He locked the boy away in the palace, behind high walls.

All the boy was permitted to see was wealth and beauty.

But the gods toppled the king's plans.

They un-locked the gates to the palace and led the boy beyond the walls, to the world outside.

There he saw four visions:

An old man, wrinkled with age.
And Prince Siddhartha learned he would grow old.

A sick person, suffering from disease.
And Prince Siddhartha learned he would grow sick.

A corpse.
And Prince Siddhartha learned of the inevitability of death.

Finally, he was shown an ascetic, a traveling monk.
And the prince realized wealth and beauty meant nothing.

Siddhartha had glimpsed his best self.
The person he was inside.

The next morning, the prince left his palace.
He brought no belongings but the clothes on his back.
He took the first steps down a path of his own.

Awareness is all.
Do not try to hide from yourself.
Your feelings exist, including fear and anger.
Recognize that life is more than a walled palace.
It is a vast overwhelming landscape, filled with mystery.
This is a step towards joy.

CHAPTER 2

Own Your Choices

Reframe everything you do as a conscious choice.
You make choices every day.
Own them.

You are not obligated to please your friends.
You choose to have these friends.
You can call your own shots.

You are not "trapped" in a relationship.
You choose to be with a partner.
You can leave.

You are not stuck in a dead-end job.
You choose to do that work.
You can walk away.

There are limits to choice. Some things are beyond your control.
You don't choose to have a disease.
But you choose how to deal with the situation.

You can take a positive approach to illness, accept your range of feelings and treat yourself with love.

You don't ask to be born poor, but even with poverty you have choices.

You are not a victim of fate.

Life brings you good and bad, mostly at random.

The future consists of a range of predictable events - a bell curve of things that could happen.

At one end, you could win the lottery, or be born with a unique talent or terrific looks. These outcomes are rare, but they occur.

On the other end of the curve, you could be born in poverty or with a physical disability.

Most outcomes fall in the middle of the curve. They constitute the daily routine of your life.

But - as they say on Wall Street - past performance is no guarantee of future return.

You will eventually hit the tails of the curve. Don't let them take you by surprise.

Someone you know - or you - will:

Contract an illness.

Die in an accident.

Lose a job.

Earn a million dollars.

Become famous.

Go bankrupt.

These are predictable events.

When something bad happens, there is no crisis.

There is no such thing as a crisis.

You cannot steer luck, but you can expect a range of good and bad outcomes.

You make choices based on what you get.

Stephen Jay Gould, a professor at Harvard, taught me this lesson.

I took Gould's course three years after he was diagnosed with abdominal mesothelioma, a deadly cancer. With his usual courage, Gould lectured about his experience and related it to the science of statistics.

Gould's doctors termed his cancer hopeless and gave him eight months to live. He prepared his affairs and set up trusts for his family, but also applied his scientific mind to the question of how long he might actually survive.

These investigations revealed a bell curve that described his chances – and like all bell curves, it had narrow tails at either end.

In all likelihood, he would fall into the middle of the curve, and die quickly, about eight months after diagnosis.

On the other hand, there was a distant chance he'd end up in one of those tails and die the next morning, or many years in the future.

As things turned out, Stephen Jay Gould survived twenty years after his diagnosis.

This was no miracle.

If you examine the scientific evidence, the outcome was predictable. Gould knew there was a chance he'd survive for many years, so he prepared himself for it, just as he prepared for the more likely case that he'd die far sooner.

Understanding the range of foreseeable outcomes gave him a measure of control amid difficult circumstances.

Don't be surprised when the unexpected happens. It is foreseeable.

I was walking to work one morning in 2001 when an airliner flew into a skyscraper three blocks away.

It could happen and it did.

The only certainty is change.
Stability is an illusion, not a goal.
Life is not stable.
It never will be.

The events in your life fall into two categories:
Things you don't control - governed by a bell curve of foreseeable outcomes.
Things you do control - a series of choices you make for yourself.
The serenity prayer sums it up:
God grant us the serenity to accept the things we cannot change,
courage to change the things we can,
and wisdom to know the difference.

The things out of your control are predictable. They are out there, and some of them will happen.
The things you can change – that's where you can take charge.

If you refuse to own choices, you become a martyr.
Suffering to attract attention.
A workaholic sits at his desk, hoping everyone else will notice.
If you put his message into words, it sounds like this:
"Notice me! I'm not being cared for! I do everything. No one takes care of me!"
Not so different from a screaming infant.
Martyrs enjoy discharging their unconscious anger.
An infant letting out a nice loud scream.
There's a better way.

Ask for help. Point out when others need to do their part. Admit you enjoy working hard.

If you seek recognition, ask for a raise. Request a promotion. Get another job.

Take care of yourself.

You're not an infant.

Don't do anything you are going to resent.

It's not worth it.

Own your choices, and there's nothing to resent.

Don't be a charity martyr.

Donate to good causes, volunteer your time - but do it for yourself.

Feel generous, get your name on the donor list.

It's a choice. Own it.

After college, I worked as a social worker with foster children.

People told me I was a good person.

I said no, I enjoy it. I like kids and driving all over the city visiting foster moms.

It was fun.

I ran a volunteer program at a community center and gave my volunteers the same speech.

No one notices dramatic acts of sacrifice.

Only do this if you think you're going to like it.

The collapse fantasy is the ultimate martyr trip, a voyage back to infant helplessness.

You might not remember, but when you were an infant, someone attended to your every need. Going to the bathroom required no prior arrangement. You let loose, and someone took care of it. Eating was as simple as screaming until someone brought you a warm breast.

Life is good as a newborn. Everything is done for you. No one wants anything. You just lie there and look cute and everyone cuddles and coos.

All is well.

Nowadays, when things aren't going your way, it is tempting to regress to the old days, drop all cares and return to blessed infancy.

That's a choice.

My college roommate had a collapse fantasy that played out over exam period.

He fell ill and disappeared into his room, emerging periodically to gaze at nothing with sad eyes and radiate misery.

I'd had enough and asked what was going on.

He was a martyr, sacrificing his very being for his education. Now he was too sick to stand up.

I pointed out he was making a choice.

No one made him work so hard – he did so of his own free will. This guy was conceited about his abilities, and ultra-competitive, and he wanted to blow the rest of us away.

Getting sick was a choice, too - his way of communicating suffering.

It turned out that, as a kid, his mother spoiled him when he got sick – made him chicken soup and tucked him into bed. He missed that care, so he studied all night and deprived himself of sleep until he made himself ill. Then he expected his college roommates to act like his mother.

As this choice became conscious, he began to feel silly.

Shedding the collapse fantasy and returning to the land of the living left my roommate more time to study. He also found a few hours to watch Star Trek and eat pizza with the rest of us.

The most common collapse fantasy is the "nervous breakdown."

Some of my patients have ended up in mental hospitals when they didn't belong there - usually as teenagers. They were too young to comprehend the reality of a mental hospital, or see the consequences of their choice to check themselves into one.

At that age, my fantasy of hospitalization for a nervous breakdown was attractive too. I pictured an English country house with a large garden. A kindly nurse wheels me beneath an elm tree in a wicker wheelchair. I sit with a blanket on my lap, sip tea and gaze over the expanse of lawn.

Friends and family, hearing of my plight, hurry to visit, and murmur in hushed tones. Just rest, they say, concentrate on feeling better.

That was my collapse fantasy.

In the real world, mental hospitals aren't nice places to visit. They're filled with crazy people – genuine crazy people, who hear voices and suffer from delusions and all the horrors of serious mental illness. Luxury is non-existent, and the staff is busy helping folks with actual problems.

A stay at a mental hospital isn't relaxing, or pretty and you don't want to collapse there. Most of my patients talked their way out ASAP.

The same goes for substance abuse rehab facilities. Most aren't posh in the least – not like the fancy places designed for movie stars – and wherever you go for rehab, they cannot keep you sober. That's something you have to do for yourself, each and every day.

Own your choices. Take care of yourself. No one is better equipped.

The ne plus ultra of martyr fantasies is suicide - sacrificing yourself utterly to punish those who fail to provide you with sufficient care.

Most people who commit suicide are mentally ill and desperately unhappy, and I do not make light of their pain.

But when the inner martyr is in control, you might entertain suicidal thoughts. You might go so far as to make vague threats and drop hints.

There's no real suicidal intent - you're playing with the fantasy.

Like all martyr fantasies, these sorts of suicidal threats are outlets for unconscious anger. They are designed to hurt the people who care for you, because their care feels insufficient.

Perhaps you've imagined your funeral. All those people weeping and sobbing, wishing they'd known how much you were suffering so they could have saved you.

It is gratifying to imagine everyone who would be left behind, bereft and regretful.

The suicide fantasy amounts to acting in on unconscious anger.

You disappear to hurt everyone left behind. A victory through defeat.

It's like Masada, the walled city in Israel where the inhabitants, under siege by a Roman army, committed mass suicide. The Romans marched in triumphantly to find only corpses.

It must have felt good, at some level, for the inhabitants of Masada to exact this revenge on their tormentors, even as they died, defeated.

I suspect they were also exacting unconscious revenge on their god, who failed to protect them from the Roman attack. Since their god – a projection of an idealized father figure - wasn't there for them, they killed themselves, hurting him in the process.

Not the first time someone has hurt himself to get his parent's attention.

Don't be a martyr. Hurting yourself hurts others.
You're only acting-in on anger.
And making others angry.
Take charge of your choices instead.

Another step towards joy.

CHAPTER 3

Emotions Are Real

There are five basic emotions. You can argue over the precise number, but I've never seen a list of more than eight, and five seems about right.

Their names are words you learned in grade school:

Anger. Fear. Caring. Hurt. Happiness.

Every other word you use to describe what's going on in your head refers to either:

A cognitive rather than an emotional state, or;

A variation on these basic five.

Cognitive states refer to thoughts, not feelings.

You might feel confused right now, but confusion is not an emotion.

When you are confused, your cognition is scattered. You might be feeling afraid or hurt. Maybe you are confused because you are overwhelmed by happiness.

But the confusion itself pertains to your thoughts, not your feelings.

Similar words, such as puzzled, pensive, reflective, amazed and fascinated also describe cognitive states.

Some words you use to describe emotions merely minimize or intensify the same basic feeling state.

Annoyed means mildly angry. So do frustrated, irritated and piqued.

If you turn up the dial, you reach outraged, flabbergasted or furious.

All are variations of anger, one of the five basic emotions.

The variations only express a range of intensity. It's all the same feeling.

Petrified means more afraid. Nervous means less afraid.

Both words mean you're afraid.

Emotions are simple, yet they manage to elude your conscious mind.

This is due to a quirk of brain anatomy.

Your emotions don't live with you, in the part of your brain that contains your conscious self, but in a separate, more primitive region – the unconscious.

The human brain has three discrete parts:
An inner reptile brain.
A middle paleo-mammalian brain; and
An outer, distinctly human portion on top.
This tripartite structure reflects the path of human evolution.

The inner brain was the first to evolve, and exists in a similar form in many lower animals. It is the reptile brain because something like it exists in a lizard's head.

This brain handles tasks suitable for a reptile – basic stuff like moving and breathing.

The reptile brain also happens to be where anger and fear reside. There's an almond-sized region near the center, called the amygdala, which releases the chemicals you know as your two most fundamental emotions.

Anger or fear translate for a reptile into fight or flight.

A lizard can express anger – jump, hiss and bare its teeth — or it can express fear and flee the scene.

Your lizard brain contains what you need to lash out in fury – or flee, terrified.

We all have days like that.

The middle, paleo-mammalian brain contains the other three emotions.

The two highest and best – caring and happiness.

And the most devastating – hurt.

This portion of the brain evolved with the appearance of mammals, and so these emotions relate to the task of raising young.

There is no childcare in the reptile world. There are many off-spring, and less is invested in each individual.

A lizard lays a clutch of eggs. When they hatch, the mother might eat a few of the children or merely wander off and forget they exist.

Mammals don't lay eggs. With live young there are fewer off-spring.

When a mammal mother – let's say a dachshund – gives birth to a few puppies, she stays with them, licking and nudging them as they squirm over to her nipples so they can feed on her milk.

Instead of eating them – or forgetting them – she feels emotional tugs that keep her present on the scene.

Something in her mammalian brain says, stop – these are your children, care for them, love them, find happiness in caring for them, or hurt if they leave you before you are ready to detach your maternal bonds.

That's caring, and happiness and hurt.

The final three emotions.

The third part of the brain is the outer cortex.

It doesn't contain any emotions. It contains thoughts.

The cortex is the biggest, most sophisticated part of the brain, and it is unique to humans. The thinking you lives there, the conscious self.

As René Descartes said, "Cogito, ergo sum."

I think, therefore I am.

When you stop thinking, and begin feeling, you return to the primitive, interior regions of your brain. This is your evolutionary past, where survival instincts pre-date language and consciousness.

The cortex doesn't expect emotions. It is puzzled by paleo-mammalian impulses of caring, happiness and hurt, and nearly overwhelmed by the forces of fear and anger welling up from the reptile brain. It does its best to dismiss the storm of emotion within, and escape into thought.

You are your cortex.

You are more comfortable talking about thoughts than emotions. You resist examining feelings before going into action.

To make matters worse, emotions arrive from the inner brain in a tangled, contradictory welter.

If emotions obey a rule, it's Newton's Third Law of Motion.

For every force, there is an equal and opposite force.

It's like the old song:

Sometimes I love you.

Sometimes I hate you.

But when I hate you.
It's 'cause I love you.

Countervailing feelings constantly vie for your attention. Love and anger form two sides of the same coin – and sadness arrives sprinkled with elation.

Walt Whitman wrote:

Do I contradict myself?
Very well then I contradict myself,
(I am large, I contain multitudes.)

Emotionally, we all contradict ourselves, and contain multitudes.

You identify emotions by putting your experience into words. That's the basis for talk therapy. Writing works too – keeping a journal or writing letters.

A patient of mine who was a music therapist used to express his feelings to me by improvising on a flute and a dulcimer. Music is another language that expresses emotion, just like dance, or the visual arts.

The key is to translate emotion into language form. That sends signals from the inner brain where emotion resides to the language centers in the cortex.

There you can examine your feelings consciously.

The process creates awareness, and permits the best self to emerge.

Loss is a trigger for contradictory emotions.

One of my patients had a friend who was gravely ill.

I asked him to talk, to put what he was feeling into words.

Initially, he was conscious only of sadness at the approaching death of his friend. But as he kept talking, other, more troubling emotions emerged.

There was anger at his friend's demands for attention.

Relief that the end was approaching.

Hurt that after providing so much care, he himself would be abandoned.

Fear that his friend's coming death presaged his own.

The usual welter of conflicting human feelings.

You cannot push "wrong" emotions out of your thinking mind. They will catch up with you when your unconscious mind takes over – like when you try to sleep.

There is no should with emotions, only what you feel.

Should is your cortex trying to converse logically with a lizard and a dachshund.

Your feelings can be illogical, irrational, and contradictory. You can't control what you feel, but you can comprehend your emotions so they don't control you.

Own all your feelings, understand them.

Give yourself permission to be human.

With your unconscious mind no longer fighting for attention, you can be your best self – a more conscious self.

Living consciously, with awareness of your emotions, is a pathway to joy.

CHAPTER 4

Depression

Refusing to own anger causes depression.

Depression is not feeling sad. Sadness is an emotion, a variety of hurt. It coexists with other feelings, and can be owned and understood.

You might enjoy sitting with a bit of sadness, like savoring the bittersweet nostalgia of thumbing through old photographs on a rainy day.

Each emotion arrives accompanied by countervailing emotions.

Sadness often trails a whiff of happiness in its wake.

Depression is different. It is caused by bottled anger: forgetting you are a self-reliant adult and regressing into patterns from early childhood – a helpless, dependent state in which pleasing others is the primary survival strategy.

At first glance, anti-depressant drugs seem like the simplest solution for depression. For that reason, they have become ubiquitous.

I haven't tried these drugs myself, but a number of my patients have used them, and their experiences vary.

Some said they felt relief from painful feelings. Others didn't think the drugs made much difference. Some found the medications compressed their range of feeling, reducing the depths of the lows, but also bringing down emotional highs. Some objected to the side-effects these drugs produce. Others found that the medication brought them to a place where they were more receptive to psychotherapy, calming them and making it easier to talk. Several of my patients have discontinued medication after working with me for a time, feeling that they no longer needed it to help them control their depression.

There is a built-in draw-back to anti-depressant medication: the benefits only appear if you keep taking the pills. If you wish to rely solely on medication to control your feelings, then you must remain on these drugs for the rest of your life.

Physical exercise is a good alternative. Exercise is healthy and has the effect of administering a natural medication with no side effects. An increased heart-rate triggers the production of endorphins, your body's own built-in anti-depressants.

I encourage my patients to stay active, for their body and their spirit.

But to address the root cause of depression you have to put your anger into words.

Re-claiming your right to anger marks a return to adulthood, and will result in the lifting of depression. If you locate and express what you're feeling, you will find a ladder out of the well, and back to the land of the living.

The problem is that depressed people are determined not to express their anger. It feels like a matter of life and death to them to deny angry feelings.

That's because it once was – when they were young children.

Anger is so forbidden to a depressed person that the absence of appropriate anger is a fool-proof sign of depression.

Ask a depressed person if he's angry:

Only at myself.

But anger at oneself is circular. It makes no logical sense.

You are you, and you determine who you are each and every moment you exist.

You can't select your own skills or talents, or how you look.

But skills and talents and appearance are not what matters.

It's that you tell the truth – are authentically present, as your best self.

If you don't like yourself, you can change that in an instant, and be more authentic – be your best self.

The depressed person only turns his anger within and self-attacks because he has no other permissible object.

This turning in of anger results in the second symptom of depression: low self-esteem.

A depressed person doesn't like who he is. Like a young child relating to a disapproving parent, he seeks only to please.

If his attempt fails, he self-attacks.

A child is designed to please adults, and is helpless without adult support.

When a young child is punished, he can only blame himself. He has failed in his purpose. The fault can only lie within him.

Under stress, a depressed person regresses into that helpless child. Instead of fighting back, he locates the fault within, and self-attacks.

Evolution explains why young children locate the fault within.

All higher animals, when very young, must please their parents. They do so in order to receive care.

The young animal who best pleases his parents is most likely to survive and pass the adaptation along to the next generation.

Human children, like other young animals, are parent-delighting machines.

They have to be to survive.

The new-born bird who attracts his parent's positive attention will get more worms.

In fact, in many bird species, if there is insufficient food to feed a large brood, the parents will cull their young by pushing one or more of them over the edge of the nest to fall to their death. Some waterfowl will drown their young, or chase them away and deny them food until they weaken and perish.

A superior ability to please adults could mean the difference between life and death.

It is no coincidence that cartoon creatures you find "cute" bear the physical characteristics of newborn animals – a disproportionately large head and eyes and rounded, softened body features.

Identifying something as cute means you feel a tug to take care of it, that it is helpless and needing your aid.

For a young child, failing to be cute risks catastrophe.

If a young child fails to please a parent, he must make himself more parent-pleasing.

A young child removed from an abusive home often asks to be returned. This makes sense in his world. Survival depends upon the presence of a parent. Even a neglectful or abusive parent is preferable to abandonment.

Even a stranger, if he is an adult, remains a figure of authority in the eyes of a young child. If a stranger slaps a young child for no reason, that child, lacking other guidance, will locate the blame within himself. He will not know why he was punished. He will intuit he did something wrong.

The younger the child, the stronger the impulse to locate the fault within.

An adult can address others as equals.

He can fight back, and express anger at mistreatment.

A child focuses on pleasing. If he fails to please, he must become more pleasing.

This is the pattern of depression.

Stress triggers depression. You regress back into a child. You relate to the world as a child relates to adults.

The world becomes overwhelming, all-powerful.

Your instinct is to locate the fault within.

You lose the adult ability to relate to the world as an equal.

You become a child who has failed to please.

You self-attack.

Self-esteem drops.

You sink into despair.

You may generalize your feelings, too, as children do.

Everyone will seem unhappy.

A world around you devoid of joy.

To treat depression, you must return to adult functioning. That begins with locating your anger.

This is not to say you will always be right.

It is saying you are not always wrong.

You have a right to live as your best self, and to defend that self against abuse.

You have a right to be you, and to like who you are.

The re-framing question helps beat depression. It is designed to force you to think like an adult, not a child – to find the anger, and to find out why you are angry.

The re-framing question is simple:

Would I have done to that person what he did to me?

A re-working of the Golden Rule – also intended to create empathy and perspective.

To bring out the best self.

Find something that ought to make you angry.

If you are depressed, this is harder than it sounds. A depressed person feels no right to anger, only a numbness where the anger should be, and a deep self-disgust.

You might resort to politics.

Get angry at the president, the mayor, your boss or the weather. Anything that isn't fair and ought to be different will do the trick.

Ask the re-framing question.

Would I do to him what he did to me?

No one is perfect.

There are two sides to every story.

But if someone hurt you and you are being your best self, you wouldn't have done it to him. The answer will be no.

The re-framing question reminds you that you are an adult, a person with a right to an opinion, a right to disagree – a right to anger.

My patient, Marta, came to me with depression. She was dating someone for three perfect months when he stopped calling.

Marta finally asked for an explanation, and he said it wasn't working for him.

That was that.

Now Marta wept in my office, so depressed she dreaded each day and wished she could disappear into the ground.

I asked if she was angry at how she'd been treated.

No.

Only at myself.

This is my pattern.

They always reject me sooner or later. I'm a worthless, clingy loser.

The re-framing question:

Would she have treated this guy the way he treated her?

Marta was stumped. She wanted to say yes, but hesitated. She knew it wasn't true. Deep down, in her best self, Marta was a kind person, and she didn't consciously treat people cruelly.

I probably deserved what I got. He has a right not to want me in his life.

Again, the re-framing question:

Would she have treated this guy the way he treated her?

She mulled it over and finally admitted the obvious.

No, I wouldn't. Not like that. Not the way he did it.

I asked her why.

Because I've been there. I know how much it hurts. I know you need a little consideration, a kind word, an explanation. After three months, he didn't even say goodbye. It didn't have to be like that.

I noticed a change in her expression. The real Marta was returning.

How do you feel about someone treating you like that?

Marta hesitated.

Well, I don't understand it.

That's cognitive. Give me a feeling.

Then I guess it makes me sad.

I regarded her skeptically.

Someone treats you inconsiderately and it only makes you sad?

She smiled.

Okay. It also makes me angry.

The real Marta began to speak.

I don't care how needy or hopeless someone is. No one deserves to be dumped without a phone call. We were together three months. He doesn't have to date me, but he could have sat down to talk. It didn't have to be like this.

Marta was back in the room. We had more to do, but she'd expressed her anger, like an adult. Her depression had lifted, just a bit.

She'd stopped locating the fault within. Now there were two sides to the story.

Claim your anger. It will relieve depression.
Another step forward to joy.

CHAPTER 5

Reparenting

The re-framing question knocks you out of the regression that causes depression. It reawakens the adult.

But you can't ignore the child. When you are unconscious he's you.

We have to understand him, find out what he wants and why.

If you ignore your child, he'll cry louder and appear when you least want him.

Better to sit him down at the table, like an adult, and ask him what's wrong.

This is the work of re-parenting.

The old joke about psychotherapy is that it just gets you angry at your parents.

It sounds like a punch-line, but there's truth in it.

Psychotherapy is about awareness. The first piece of awareness is the fact of your anger. The earliest object for anger will be your parents – the first people you ever knew, who were once all-powerful rulers of your world.

It isn't the present you who's angry. It is the child holding grudges from the past.

It isn't your present parents he's angry at. The child is angry at the past parents, the people he experienced when you were small and helpless and they were like gods.

That, in a nutshell, is why you still harbor anger at your parents.

To you, they're who they were.

To them, they're who they are.

The goal is not to blame. The goal is to explain.

Sometimes, it isn't even your parents you're thinking about when you discuss your parents.

It's the notion of parents. The idea of parents.

A powerful concept. One that triggers feelings from deep in your past, deep in our collective past. Dependency. Deprivation. Longing. A craving for care.

These feelings are innate to your being. They exist at a cellular level.

Your child is angry because your parents failed at the task of raising you. Not entirely, but to some degree.

That's because parenting is an impossible task.

No one can ever be the perfect parent for another person – only for himself.

You have a right to that anger, as you have a right to all your anger. Of course you loved your parents – every child does. But love and anger coexist.

Some parents fail profoundly at the task of parenting. The physical, emotional and sexual abuse of children is real.

But even a good parent, a caring parent who tries his best, will fail to some degree. All parents are in some way, and to some extent, bad parents, and all parenting is bad parenting. The best parents are good enough.

Freud called psychotherapy the "impossible profession," but parenting is worse. It is an impossible job. Unless you look at parenting realistically, as an impossible task, it is doomed to failure from the start.

No human being can match the ideal of the parent you long for, so you are bound to be disappointed and desire to change the parents you have.

The true task of parenting is guiding a child through his disappointment in you for not being perfect.

Coming of age is realizing your parents are human and frail and mortal.

You will separate from them to take care of yourself.

And maybe take care of them.

This sounds harsh, but at an existential level, parenting is harsh. A parent introduces a helpless infant to the fact of mortality. By admitting he is human, he models acceptance of the human condition.

A good parent admits he will fail the child, but will always accept him as he is.

A good parent does the best he can until the child learns the necessity of caring for himself.

Behind the task of parenting lies the illusion of stability. Children thrive on stability, and good parents can maintain the illusion for years.

The school bus arrives at 8:00 am.

Dinner is served at 6:00 p.m.

Everything starts out predictable the way kids like it.

Behind the scenes, the parent struggles to shelter the child from reality, the instability that exists outside in the adult world where people lose jobs, marriages break up and there are no guarantees that things will stay the same for long.

Eventually, the parent must introduce the child to the real world – an unpredictable, unstable place.

The process I call re-parenting is about learning to care for yourself by returning to repair the parenting of your child-self. It involves returning to your childhood and replaying points in time when your parents failed to give you the support you needed to separate and go out on your own.

You return to re-parent yourself, and this time you get it right.

As an adult, you access a spectrum of feeling a child cannot comprehend. You wrest back control and understand events as they happened, with your full, adult range of emotion.

You have a storehouse of childhood memories. For this exercise, we will choose an archetypal example of a parent planting a negative voice into a young child. This is the genesis of all the nagging thoughts that there's something wrong with who you are.

Here's the scenario:

Imagine you're on a bus and you see a mother with a small boy, four years old, sitting across the aisle. The mother is impatient and in a fit of anger, she slaps the child.

The little boy stares in disbelief, as young children do, tears running down his face.

Everyone on the bus looks away, embarrassed, or they shake their heads and murmur under their breath as strangers do in these situations.

You are helpless to interfere. Interrupting this mother for an impromptu lecture on child-rearing would be a mistake, and only result in anger and indignation. Who are you to tell her how to raise her child?

You can only watch, and wish she hadn't hit her kid.

What you are watching is a mother doing a poor job of child-rearing, and maybe you are outraged or saddened or frustrated, or formulating an exasperated story to recount to a friend.

But you remain silent, and so does everyone else.

This scenario is iconic: a mother scolding a child who doesn't understand why he is being punished. If you search your memory for instances like this, you will find examples percolating up from the past.

I know from working with childhood memories that if you clear your head and think of a memory, any memory from your childhood, the first one that pops into your head will most likely include an interaction of this kind with a parent – one in which you were made to wonder who you were and where you stood in your parent's esteem.

These memories needn't be severe to linger like unfinished business in our minds.

Even the slight annoyance or impatience of a parent can result in a lasting memory of pain or feelings of worthlessness in a child.

Children are sensitive, they focus intently on the parent at all times, and no parent is perfect.

Now return to the bus, and use your imagination to see the world through the eyes of a child. That's where damaging voices that endure into adulthood are already beginning to form.

Step into that child.

Things look different through the eyes of a four-year old. That woman on the bus isn't just a woman, or a mother, she is The Mother, and she defines your world, your home – the universe as you know it.

An adult can tut-tut over this woman's parenting ability. The child cannot fathom such power. He will not conceive of criticizing his mother for years to come.

The child will locate the fault within.

When your mother hits you the only one conclusion is that you have done something wrong. Any suggestion that she is at fault overturns the basis of your existence, which is utter dependence on a parent.

It is no coincidence that a parent is god-like to a young child.

Religious belief is rooted in a child's need for a perfect parent. Under the stress of our own mortality, we regress to a child's belief system. If the volcano erupts, it isn't your god's fault – it must be something you, the villagers, did to displease him. You must confess. Do penance. Cleanse your sin.

The child on the bus received a staggering lesson, perhaps for the first time.

He is bad, he is capable of badness. If he is himself, seeking to please, he can still be bad. He must monitor and control the bad within him – or hide it.

He cannot trust himself.

Events like that incident on the bus may damage his confidence for a lifetime.

Re-parenting creates counter-voices to heal the child.

Love is a child's right because every child is good. He needs unconditional love like food and water.

Your child-self still carries that need.

As Allen Ginsberg, the poet, once told me:

We all want warm arms to hold us tight, and a voice to say I love you.

You want to be liked.

You hope people like you.

If this is "needy" then everyone is needy.

The problem isn't being needy, it's learning how to meet those needs.

You repair the hurt from that mother's slap by returning to that bus as an adult, accompanied by the child.

These exercises are a starting place.

You can role-play them with a therapist, write them in a journal, or use them as the basis for meditation.

I will use the bus example for illustration. You can revisit any memory. Sometimes the ones that seem to come from nowhere carry hidden meaning.

First exercise: The child as an adult.

Inhabit the body of that kid on the bus.

Speak as an adult the words you would like that boy to tell his mother.

You're an adult.

Give the boy adult thoughts.

What do you think you're doing? I'm four years old. Can't you see you're hurting me? I need love, not cruelty. Get it together. Don't take your issues out on a kid.

As an adult, you can see a wider perspective.
You know a parent shouldn't hit a child.
An adult can protect himself, and fight back.
You have the words to confront her.

Second exercise: The child as a child.
You are the child, as a child.
Tell the mother how it feels.
Speak as a child, from a child's world.

Why did you hit me? I love you. I want to love you. I want you to love me. I want to please you. You are my world. What did I do wrong? Do you still love me? What did I do wrong? Don't you still love me? I love you. I love you.

A child wants to be loved.
Just like you.
Feel how vulnerable that child is – how deep his need for love.
That's still a part of who you are.

Third exercise: Speak to the child
You are an adult. A friend.
Kneel beside the child on the bus.
Soothe his hurt.
Address the child.

It's going to be okay. Your mother loves you. You did nothing wrong. The person inside you is good. She's in a bad mood. She made a mistake, but you are strong. You will be okay. You did nothing wrong.

Don't forget to say:
I love you.

The child needs to hear your love. Put your arms around him.
Say those words.
You still need that.
You are still that child.

Fourth exercise: Be the parent.
Step into the parent.
Be the parent this child needs.
The one he deserves.
Talk to the boy.

I love you. You are beautiful. You are my boy. You are what is best in me. I celebrate myself through you, my precious gift. You are all good, you carry my love always. You are my son. I love you as I love myself. I cherish you within my heart.

This is the ideal parent voice.
You may never have heard it before.
But you need to carry it within if you are to heal.
You deserve to hear it every day.
It helps you to love yourself.
To find your best self.

In re-parenting you offer yourself the love and care you needed but did not receive as a child. You accept the child you were and the person you are.
Soothing your child is healing yourself.
A step towards joy.

CHAPTER 6

Expectation and Predictions

You predict the outcome of present events based on the past.

It happened last time, so unconsciously, you expect it to happen again.

This ignores reality.

Ivan Pavlov performed an experiment with dogs at the turn of the twentieth century. He rang a bell, then gave the dogs food.

Eventually, ringing the bell made the dogs salivate, expecting their dinner.

Here's another example:

You walk into a room filled with strangers.

You experience instantaneous, unconscious responses to each of these other people. Just as everyone else in the room does.

I like that woman – she has a friendly face.

That one looks angry, I'll avoid him.

He's a snob, I can tell from the way he sits.

I get a bad vibe from her. We won't get along.

Each person will have broader responses, too:
Feel an impulse to win the room over.
Decide to lay low.
Hope for silence.
Pray someone starts talking.

I leave my therapy group in silence sometimes. Observe their reactions.
Some find it soothing.
Others seem panicked.

The responses you have to strangers are based upon predictions.
Like Pavlov's dogs, you have past experiences with other, similar people.
You make new predictions based on those outcomes. You expect what happened last time to happen again.
Your predictions might be accurate.
But this unconscious process can lead to critical mistakes.

In daily life, you meet a new person and make assumptions.
You compare that person with someone in your past. This comparison drives your response.
Maybe he reminds you of an authority figure who encouraged and supported you.
You try to sound intelligent, and mention your accomplishments.
Or you might have a negative response. Maybe he reminds you of someone you disliked as a kid.
You clam up and avoid him.
You are not relating consciously to the person.

You are relating unconsciously to your past.

When you respond very strongly to someone you barely know, that response is likely based on past experience, not present reality.

Predictions affect your relationships with everyone around you – employers, romantic partners, women, men, children, black people, French people, tall people – the entire world.

Racism, homophobia, sexism, ageism.

Unconscious prejudices are predictions based on past experience.

Ask someone for the origin of a strong bias. He will relate a story of a past negative interaction.

Maybe a French person was rude to him.

He was cursed at by an African-American person.

A tall person treated him condescendingly.

Now he confuses everyone in that group with that original person. He makes a negative prediction based on the past.

This is an inappropriate response to someone you don't know.

Mostly, you relate to the world the way you related in your family.

In a roomful of strangers, the person who clams up probably clammed up in his family, too.

The person who is warm and outgoing probably still plays that role at family get-togethers.

As a child, your family is your world. You adapt to survive there.

Those adaptations live on.

Maybe you had a distant father, disapproving and hard to please. You adapted to lay low, and avoid interactions.

Now, at the workplace, you expect your boss to relate to you the way your father did, and you employ the same adaptation – laying low and avoiding interactions.

If your father was warm and supportive, you might have adapted to be outgoing and confident.

You predict your boss will respond with warmth and support, and so you utilize the old adaptation of outgoing confidence.

This pattern affects your relations with others besides your boss – friends, partners, even strangers.

Predictions based on the past affect your interactions with the world.

Living things often respond to one environment with an adaptation that would lead to disaster in another.

A duck adapts to life on water by developing webbed feet. They're not much use for running on dry land.

Acting loud and bossy might help you survive in your family. It might not succeed as a strategy at the office.

Examine the predictions you bring to relationships. You will learn about yourself, your history – and how you related to mom and dad.

I often watch a patient interact with me as a therapist, and guess how he was raised.

That's how psychics, fortune-tellers and palm-readers do their job. They draw conclusions from your dress and body language. But mostly, they base their guesses about you on how you respond to them. This provides the key to your past.

It can be tricky. Some kids imitate behavior. Others react against it.

An aggressive parent might produce a child who fights back.

Or a meek, passive survivor.

But your childhood world trains your adult responses. You think you know what's going to happen because that's what happened before.

Just like Pavlov's dogs.

Acting on unconscious predictions traps you in a loop.

You adapted to life with your parents. Now you seek a similar environment, where your adaptation will be useful.

That environment feels comfortable. You know what to expect, so you can handle it. But it might not be where you belong.

Minik the Eskimo, a seven-year-old orphan, was brought to New York City from Greenland in 1897. An American family adopted him.

Minik wanted to go home.

At nineteen, he returned to Greenland and struggled to re-learn his language and the basic skills to hunt and survive.

He failed, nearly starved, and returned to New York.

Minik longed for Greenland, because it was what he'd adapted to.

Instead of embracing possibilities in his new home, he fled to a place where he no longer belonged so he could continue to utilize old adaptations.

Like Minik, you adapt to your childhood conditions. Later in life you unconsciously seek those same conditions.

Sometimes they aren't what you need.

I learned this lesson many years ago as a member of a psychotherapy group.

We were taught to ask for what we wanted from the other members.

I arrived, beat up from a bad day at work, and told the group I needed care.

The therapist asked who I'd like to give me this care.

I chose Ronald.

Lauren, in the chair beside me, responded with hurt and anger. She'd always cared for me, and supported me in the group.

But I chose Ronald.

Ronald hated me. He grew up with learning disabilities, and I was a straight-A student. Based on his past, Ronald predicted someone like me would look down on him. As a result, he disliked me intensely.

But I grew up with a withholding, hard to please father. Chasing Ronald felt familiar. I'd adapted to chasing people who didn't like me. I wanted love from a person like dad. So I pursued people like Ronald.

Lauren was right. It was a mistake.

She could provide me with care. Ronald couldn't.

She wanted to help me. He didn't.

I learned my lesson.

Don't run to Ronald. Go to where the care is.

You don't have to follow the loop.

You don't have to run to Ronald, or flee, like Minik, to what is familiar.

If it's not what's best for you, stay away from it.

This pattern plays out a lot with people's choices of partners.

You find a partner like mom because she feels familiar. She's what you grew up with. You adapted to mom, so you feel you belong there.

Even if you don't.

If your mother was chilly and distant, you find a partner who is chilly and distant. A warm and caring partner would be unfamiliar. She would make you anxious.

You're used to chilliness. Like Pavlov's dogs, you expect it, based on past experience. Better to have the chilliness now, so you can deal with it.

Except it doesn't have to come. That's just a prediction, based on past events.

Past adaptations often harden until they merge with self-image and become an aspect of who you think you are. They can seem immutable.

My patient, Juan, insisted he was shy.

As a small child, his mother brought him to her friends' parties.

Juan chattered and performed – an excited, happy little boy.

When the parties ended, his mother turned angry and dissected Juan's every move: He'd made a fool of himself. He'd embarrassed her.

This cycle happened several times, until Juan learned to be shy.

He grew cautious. Averted his eyes. Mumbled. Only spoke when spoken to.

Years later, Juan still avoided social settings.

But Juan wasn't shy. He never was.

A small child adapted to an environment in order to survive.

That environment was long gone, but the old adaptation – representing old predictions about the world around him – remained.

The "shyness" no longer protected Juan. It stunted, sabotaged and stifled his personality.

Flexibility, and a willingness to change, was essential to overcoming this old pattern and letting him be the person he really was.

But trained responses are difficult to alter.

Once you've drummed in that the bell brings food, you can't expect the dog not to drool. He will connect that sound to the taste of supper for a long time.

Respect these old patterns. Even as you shed them, remember your life once depended upon them.

In New York City, Minik would seem crazy smearing whale fat on his body.

In Greenland it may have saved his life.

In my therapy group, going to Ronald for care seemed nuts.

But as a child, I had to believe I could somehow win my father's approval.

For Juan, shutting down and avoiding others left him isolated and miserable.

Many years earlier, it permitted a little boy to survive his mother's attacks.

You cling to old adaptations. They're tough to break, and regression is part of recovery.

Stress only adds to the problem, since when you're under pressure, or anxious, you tend to regress into old, unconscious behavior.

The ancient Taoist philosopher, Lao-Tzu, said:

A journey of a thousand miles begins with a single step.

Give yourself time to readjust, readapt and move on.
Awareness brings change.

Examine the life you are leading.   Spot the old,
unconscious predictions.
Addressing these patterns is a step towards joy.

CHAPTER 7

Anxiety

People visit therapists for two reasons, depression and anxiety.

Regressing into child-think creates depression.

Old predictions create anxiety.

If something bad happened in the past, you predict it will happen again.

So you rush to get it over with.

There is a paradox in the way anxiety works. You scare yourself to soothe yourself.

Scary unconscious thoughts don't seem soothing.

But surprise is what you dread above all else.

Every animal does. You'd rather be anxious than surprised.

Being prepared for the worst is better than having it come at you unawares.

The element of surprise transforms fear into terror.

Movie directors know what scares people. They keep it dark – monsters lurk in shadows. The camera follows the actor, so you can't see what's behind him.

Knowing where the monsters are makes them less frightening.

You soothe your fears by assuring yourself you won't be surprised.

Some trauma victims enjoy scary movies.

I worked with a rape survivor who sat through endless slasher films. She told herself it was just Hollywood actors and fake blood. Conquering her fear calmed her.

Another patient was left alone for long periods as a child by immigrant parents unable to afford childcare. He spent terrified hours in a shadowy playpen. Now he's obsessed with monster movies. He enjoys assuring himself he isn't scared.

This is the principle behind nightmares. The unconscious mind calms itself by playing out your worst fears while you sleep. If the worst has happened, there are no more surprises.

You would rather see what terrifies you.

Than dread what lurks in the shadows.

Fear evolved early.

Tiny lizards have to be alert for predators.

But they need to feel safe sometimes too.

To curl up in their dens and let the fear wash out of their brains.

So do humans.

Problems develop, in animals and humans, when you experience too much fear for too long a time. It becomes difficult to wind down to a relaxed state.

Post-Traumatic Stress Disorder was discovered among soldiers in the First World War, who spent months living in combat trenches. The constant trauma of battle never permitted them to flush out their fear. This produced debilitating neurological problems.

You don't have to survive trench warfare to suffer the effects of fear.

Children are helpless in our adult world. If they grow up amid frightening conditions, they can suffer the effects later in life.

Some children experience horrors – physical and sexual abuse.

But even minor incidents, like a harsh rebuke or casual rejection, can leave a child disoriented and frightened, and carry effects that appear later in life.

Another case of past experience creating predictions.

If you grow up in a home that doesn't feel safe, you don't feel safe in the world.

Catastrophizing is a strategy to escape anxiety. You rush to get the worst over with. A catastrophizer predicts disaster, then hurries the process.

Some catastrophizers turn every little problem into a catastrophe so they know they won't be surprised by anything going wrong. A slight set-back gets blown up into a total disaster.

You freak out if you're running a little bit late, and predict you'll miss everything and that will trigger the end of the world.

But you're really just running a little bit late.

Other catastrophizers take something essentially good and make sure something goes wrong with it. Just to be on the safe side.

My patient, Jill, was the second kind of catastrophizer.

As a kid, she worked hard to win her mother's approval, but it never came.

If Jill got good grades, her mother would call her a show-off. If she made new friends, her mother would criticize them. In young Jill's world nothing ended well. There was always her mother's inevitable, crushing disapproval.

Jill adapted to this environment by arranging catastrophes to relieve the pressure.

She did well in school until her grades plunged.

She competed at tennis, then her playing fell apart.

She pursued a guy until things got serious, then found a way to blow it.

Even clearly positive developments, like a promotion at work, got a negative spin when she discussed them, as if to keep them from getting too good.

Jill couldn't see why she kept sabotaging her own success. She asked if I could make her stop the self-destructive pattern.

Forcing change never works. Instead, we listened to Jill's child-self, to understand her childhood world, and the logic of this adaptation.

Permitting herself to hope for success led to disaster, so Jill learned as a child to avoid anxiety by taking control over when the inevitable disaster occurred.

Less surprise meant less fear.

Now, as an adult, with no mother to tear her down, Jill was acting on auto-pilot. The unconscious pattern that once protected her served no purpose.

Over time, Jill discovered other strategies to self-soothe. She reminded herself that her predictions weren't real. She learned to take time-outs to unwind.

Disaster was not inevitable.

That was only the case when her mother ran the world.

Borderline behavior is another unconscious pattern designed to avoid anxiety. Borderlines hide from their fears until something – even a minor suspicion -- triggers panic. Then they attack with everything they've got.

This leaves them swinging back and forth between a regressed, child-like vulnerability and extreme anger. There's no middle ground.

The change can occur in a flash, and borderline behavior can be extreme and unpleasant to witness. In fact, the term "borderline" is sometimes misused as a put-down in psychology circles.

Everyone is a little bit borderline.

You long to be a trusting child.

But snap into anger when your trust is broken.

Borderline parents create borderline children.

These are the parents who fluctuate back and forth from love to anger.

First they love you unconditionally, so you let your guard down.

Then they turn on you, sending you reeling.

And then it begins again.

After a few of these pendulum swings, you start oscillating too. First running to love, then fleeing from anger. As you grow older, the pattern sets.

You thought she loved you – she was your best friend.

Then she betrayed you. She's a fake, out of your life forever.

Then the crisis passes. You wonder why you over-reacted to nothing.

Two examples of borderline parents creating the borderline pattern:

An alcoholic mother snuggles up to her son and bursts into tears, telling him she loves him, and only him, in the whole world.

Hours later, she's drunk and raging that he's worthless, an embarrassment.

A father shows patience with his daughter as she learns to ride a bicycle. She opens up to him about her fear of losing her balance, and feels understood.

Later, she overhears her father, in a fit of temper, complaining to a friend that his immature daughter still needs training wheels.

She feels betrayed – terrified, hurt and angry.

Kids seek stability. They are largely helpless, and a stable world feels safe.

When a parent's love isn't stable, it sends them reeling, anxious and uncertain of themselves.

A parent's betrayal seems to come from nowhere.

Children love unconditionally, and expect the same.

For a parent to break that trust shatters all expectations.

The child searches for the link between the loving parent and the rejecting one, and finds only the unknown. Anxiety sets in, and the oscillation begins.

He walks on egg shells, seeking love, knowing it must exist.

At a hint of betrayal, he snaps into humiliation and rage.

My patient, Lou, had a strong borderline pattern.

Lou's parents were locked in a miserable marriage. His father was gay, but hid it by dating women. This was back in the 1950's, before gay people found widespread acceptance for their relationships. When Lou's mother got pregnant, the social mores of the times dictated that his parents marry, but they were both disappointed in how their lives turned out.

As a couple, they flipped between extremes.

They could put on a show of happiness – family trips and holidays and spoiling little Lou with gifts. This was the life they wanted, and tried to convince themselves they could have together.

Then the hopelessness of their situation would reemerge during long nights of drunken screaming and hateful accusations.

Lou never knew whether his parents were going to smile and praise him, or blame him, in an alcoholic binge, for ruining their lives. He could never trust their love, because he knew there was something uglier beneath the surface, a contempt for him and one another.

When Lou came out as a gay man himself, his mother couldn't hide her disgust for the son who took after her husband. Lou's father avoided the whole topic, which was too painful and filled with shame and secrecy.

Anxiety tinged every aspect of Lou's relationships.

Hungry for the love that he had tasted but never trusted, Lou would date someone for a few weeks, and open up, sharing his need for acceptance and care.

Then some small signal that seemed wrong – a careless remark, or a failure to call him back – would send him spiraling into rage.

Lou dropped lovers and friends suddenly, with no explanation.

Making the pattern conscious, and slowing it down, permitted Lou to halt the swings back and forth and catch his breath – to stop and think before going into action.

He learned to walk a middle path, of moderation – to contain his anxiety, and test the accuracy of his unconscious impulses.

In retrospect, most of the betrayals he perceived were nothing more than misunderstandings or inadvertent rudeness.

Nothing that couldn't be talked out and resolved.

The borderline pattern is an exhausting way of life – chasing love, then running for cover, haunted by the fear that disaster will arrive, that another shoe is always ready to drop.

Like the catastrophizer, the borderline is searching for a way to hide from his greatest fear – being taken by surprise.

Anxiety is triggered by cognition: a predictive thought that something bad is going to happen.

To address anxiety, you have to address that cognition:

Identify the scary thought.

Put it into words.

Reality-test it.

Then formulate soothing counter-thoughts.

I worked with a patient named Jae, who was grinding his teeth at night.

He managed to crack two fillings.

He also suffered from gastrointestinal upset that had brought him to his doctor for colonoscopies and endoscopies and endless treatments that didn't make much difference.

Typical symptoms of anxiety.

We started our work together by identifying the predictive thought that was triggering Jae's anxiety.

He was an architect, working at a small firm.

When he'd started seeing me, years before, he was in New York City finishing his masters degree. Now we worked together via the internet, over videochat.

Jae was miserable at his job, bored with laboring over the details of roofs and windows and frustrated with living in a small, isolated city. He knew he would have to quit this job or he'd go crazy, but the architecture industry was in disarray, and he couldn't find another position.

His girlfriend was supportive, as were his parents.

But moving back to the city terrified him.

As I investigated further, it became clear that the most frightening thought to Jae was that he would sink back to his lowest point, where he'd found himself five years earlier.

At that time, Jae had been living in New York City, unemployed, drinking too much, and living off his wealthy parents' handouts.

He'd hated who he was, and felt deeply ashamed.

The thought that terrified Jae was that he would find himself in that place once again.

I asked him to enunciate the thought – to put it into words.

I don't want to end up like it was in those days. I never want to end up like that again, all alone and hating myself. It was horrible. I don't think I can stay here at this job – I'm miserable. But I freak out even thinking I could end up unemployed again and living on my parents' money. I thought I'd escaped from that nightmare, and now it seems like it's back and I can't bear it.

The next step was to reality-test the cognition.

I pointed out that Jae was a different person from the man he'd been five years before. He had the masters degree, and a year's experience as an architect. He hadn't had a drink of alcohol in five years. He had a lovely girlfriend, a financial analyst, who celebrated his successes, but also understood the challenges of his career. She participated in one of our sessions, and told him she was proud of him, knew he was working hard, and promised she was there for him through thick and thin. Jae's relationship with his parents had improved a lot, too. They had explained to him that their "handouts" to him were identical to the money they sent his two sisters. There was no stigma in accepting it. For them, it was more a matter of estate planning than charity. They saved on taxes by transferring some of their wealth to their children while they were alive. There was no hidden message in their support. They were proud of him, too.

Jae came to realize that his greatest fear – ending up back in the terrible place where he'd been five years earlier, wasn't likely to happen. He'd changed, and the situation had changed with him.

Together, we formulated counter-thoughts to address the cognition that was creating his anxiety:

I am a responsible, capable person, and a good architect.

This is a tough field, but I've found work before, and I can find work again.

Even if I have to free-lance for a while, I can still further my career.

My partner supports me and understands if I'm not earning much money. She knows I have other professional goals besides getting rich.

I am attending AA meetings, and feel confident in my ability to stay sober.

My parents support me financially, but that is their choice and they are not communicating any judgment about who I am.

I have a strong support system of people who respect me and care about me.

There is no crisis. I can leave this job, move back to New York City, take things one step at a time and enjoy my life.

These counter-thoughts, and the support of his partner, family and friends, helped Jae to make this difficult transition. In the end, he did just fine.

As is often the case, anxiety itself was the biggest problem. Jae was mostly terrified that an anxiety attack would come and paralyze him.

He was mostly afraid of being afraid.

Depression and anxiety arise from the earliest, most primitive emotions – anger and fear.

With depression, the key is owning anger, and putting it into words.

Anxiety can be more difficult to address.

Owning anger – embracing an emotion – is exhilarating.

Soothing fear – allaying an emotion – is exhausting.

And even for an adult, the world can be a scary place.

My patient, Pat, presented me with one horrifying scenario after another.

I was treating her for anxiety, and, in the pursuit of greater awareness of what was scaring her so badly, we explored her frightening thoughts.

Pat worried she would be struck down with locked-in syndrome, a medical condition in which the victim is left awake, but completely paralyzed.

I argued that the condition was very rare, and it didn't make sense to obsess over such horrors.

It turned out Pat's aunt had just contracted the condition. Pat described its effects to me in excruciating detail.

Then Pat shared her fear that an intruder would enter her apartment while she slept. That, too, had happened – recently. Despite a strong lock.

Pat was also terrified that the bus she used to commute to work would crash.

The year before it had been involved in a multi-car pile-up. She was on-board.

After listening to Pat's laundry list of horrors for a few sessions, I realized I was growing anxious, too.

I was also running out of ideas to calm her down.

Pat had identified the thoughts and enunciated them. But I was having a tough time establishing that the reality of her world differed from her predictions.

Pat's world did seem pretty scary.

I struggled to formulate soothing counter-thoughts that would effectively address Pat's fears.

She'd already tried yoga, meditation, massage and other calming practices – as well as other therapists.

It was a frustrating case.

Making Pat conscious of her thoughts only seemed to re-traumatize her.

Eventually she went on medication, which brought a measure of relief. But I return to Pat's case again and again, wondering what more I could have done to help.

I think my mistake was trying to soothe instead of facing fear head on.

Fighting back.

If you're going to deal honestly with anxiety, you have to admit your scary thoughts contain some truth. The world isn't all flowers and puppies.

Some of your predictive cognition might be correct. The reality of life can sometimes be frightening.

Aside from everything else, you're on a one-way ticket. Death awaits you, somewhere down the line.

That makes everyone start shifting in their seats.

And explains the popularity of religion, with all those soothing promises.

Let's put things in perspective, and enunciate the scariest thought of all:

Life ends with death.

There's no escaping that cognition.

But you can fight back. You don't have to surrender to your fear.

Seen realistically, death is a mundane affair. It arrives at the end of everything else. Death only becomes a distraction when you place it front and center, where it doesn't belong.

Better to make the most of what you've got while you've got it.

Life isn't all about unpleasant surprises. It's also filled with delights and wonders.

Maintaining yourself in a state of fear so you're never taken by surprise makes no sense.

Research has shown that you cannot even think clearly in an anxious state. It muddles your thoughts. Your scores on an exam will improve if you are calm and relaxed.

Anxiety, nightmares, catastrophizing, and borderline behavior are all about perpetually bracing for the other shoe to drop.

Live your life. If the shoe's going to drop – let it drop.

You can handle it.

My first partner, Adam, became sick with AIDS when I was twenty-four.

He was only twenty-seven.

There were no treatments in those days, and he endured horrors, becoming emaciated, losing his eyesight, and having to wear a diaper, which was humiliating for a young man who, months before, had been a snappy dresser.

I visited Adam in the hospital each day, and one evening as he woke from a troubled sleep, I took his hand and told him everything was going to be all right.

On the face of things, it wasn't true. Adam was young and he was dying.

In another respect, it was true. I meant it, and I felt Adam needed to hear it.

We all need to hear it.

This was nothing he couldn't handle.

Everything was going to be all right.

A few days later, Adam ended his life, painlessly, with pills.

He left when he was ready.

His photo sits on a shelf in my living room – not the dying man who spent those final weeks in a hospital bed, but the real Adam, healthy and handsome.

Everything was all right.

Adam is gone.

His suffering – and worry – are over.

This story might puzzle you.

A young man's suicide in the face of disease doesn't seem an up-lifting or soothing conclusion to a chapter on anxiety.

And maybe my telling Adam everything would be all right wasn't enough to soothe his mind.

Maybe he committed suicide as a terrified gesture of fear.

But I don't think so.

I knew my lover well enough to believe he was acting as an aware adult when he took charge of that situation, and decided to end his suffering on his own terms.

I could be wrong.

I am certain that this message – there is nothing you can't handle – is the right one. It is the only one that gets you through whatever waits out there, lying in ambush.

There is a child within you who needs soothing. He needs to know that an adult is there, someone who is in charge, who can handle anything.

That adult is also within you.

I like to think I could be that adult for Adam, and deliver a comforting message.

Ultimately, he had to be that adult for himself.

To comfort his child, take control, handle whatever came his way.

In the core of the human animal, there exists anger and fear.

Fight or flight.

The act of living is aggressive in itself.

It is a refusal to die when dying is inevitable.

Living well is a refusal to surrender to fear.

In good horror movies, there's a final act.

The victims have already been axe-murdered, or eaten.

The monster appears to be winning.

But someone remains, and she's angry.

Think of Aliens, with Sigourney Weaver wielding a super-sized flame-thrower/machine gun/rocket launcher combo.

You want to throw down with me?   Bring it, motherfucker.

The beastie can't scare you once you find your mojo.

Start fighting back.

There's nothing you can't handle.

I'll be more dignified and quote great poets.

Dylan Thomas wrote:

Do not go gentle into that good night,
Old age should burn and rave at close of day;
Rage, rage against the dying of the light.

There's no question of giving up here.

Even if the fight is hopeless, it is gratifying to release aggression.

Better to go out with a bang.

John Donne got it too:

DEATH be not proud, though some have called thee
Mighty and dreadfull, for, thou art not so...

There's more to the poem, and he cops out at the end by mentioning heaven.

(This was Jacobean England.)

But the first line says it all.

Even poets fight back.

Life seems real because it is actually happening.

An illusion because it is so short.

And disappears so completely.

Grasp it, unafraid. Keep it real and alive and yours.

The young Buddha, once he headed out on his quest to become an ascetic, sought enlightenment through meditation and yogic practices.

He sat alone, beneath a tree.

And his meditation began with three refusals directed at the world outside:

First, the refusal to move.
He sat patiently, in one spot, immobile.

Second, the refusal to breathe.
He learned to slow his breath, until he hardly needed to breathe at all.

Third, the refusal to think.
He tuned out all the distractions of the world outside, and focused only on leaving his mind blank, to wander wherever it wished.

There is a fourth refusal: the refusal to be afraid.
A peace comes from accepting this world as yours.
There's nothing in it you need to fear.

Overcome anxiety. Celebrate the good around you.
It is okay for things to be okay.

Life is a brief opportunity for joy.

PART TWO

APPLYING CONSCIOUSNESS
TO EVERYDAY LIFE

PART TWO

Applying Consciousness to Everyday Life

Patients often arrive at my office complaining of feeling "stuck."

"Stuck" means you're caught in a stasis, balanced on a fulcrum between anger and fear.

On one side, there's anger – frustration at not pursuing your dreams. You have dreams – that's what drives you forward. It is the most human thing in the world, and what makes living possible.

You know where you're headed in the end (oblivion). But you have the amazing human ability to ignore that for the time being and concentrate on a carrot dangling from a stick.

You want to chase it.

On the other side, there's fear – old predictions from your past that warn you not to take risks.

These are old voices, probably a parent's – telling you that you can't do it, that you shouldn't expose yourself to the possibility of failure.

You freeze up. Stuck.

If you want to get un-stuck, it's time to take a reckoning.

Sound daunting? Let's make it easier. Every life consists of three elements: Playing. Working. Loving.

We'll take them one at a time.

Playing: this is the toughest element to define. The name seems childish, but that's appropriate, since playing is the first challenge you tackle in life.

Even as a youngster, playing has serious aspects.

As an adult, it becomes a grab-bag: everything not working or loving – not career or relationship.

That means more than games and hobbies. It's knowing yourself alone and through others. It's friendships – people you trust and respect.

It's your support system.

Working: This is not something you do for money – it's a fundamental part of human life.

Your work reflects your essence. It is what you "do" with your life – what you leave behind you when you're gone.

To know your work, you have to know your best self.

Only you can know who you are, and what you want to do.

Loving: A relationship is a friendship, with the added benefit of attraction.

You gain an ally.

Together, you walk down a path toward a mutual goal.

People get stuck because they rush things.

The three elements have a natural order.

Playing leads you to your work.

Working instills the confidence you need to find a partner.

PLAYING

Sustaining the Contact – Creating a Support System

I've talked about unconscious regression – mostly how to prevent it.

If you live your life as a fully conscious adult instead of a child, you can take charge of the life you lead.

On the other hand, sometimes being an adult can be exhausting.

At the end of each day, you go to sleep – a regressed, unconscious state.

You cannot survive without this nightly departure from reality. Sleep deprivation is harmful, even fatal in extreme cases. It is necessary for your physical and mental health to disappear into your unconscious to rest and recover.

You also need to play.

Perhaps that's what dreams are – the play of the unconscious mind.

Conscious play – what the psychoanalyst Ernst Kris termed "regression in the service of the ego" – is also critical to staying healthy in mind and body.

It's interesting that children play at being adults.

They bang away at a miniature workbench, or play "house" or pretend to care for a doll.

They are practicing for the time when they will leave the regressed, dreamy state of childhood, and assume adult responsibilities.

Adults do just the opposite.

When you play as an adult, you regress back to childhood activities.

You might occupy yourself with sports, vegetate with a video game or disappear into a novel or a movie.

You might sit on the beach, look at a palm tree and think about the world.

A change of physical scenery can be restful.

It's nice to escape from your familiar adult world and take yourself someplace new, where no reminders exist of adult responsibilities.

You might find it useful to go somewhere without walls – and with long horizons. There's something about seeing a great distance that sets the mind to turning over new possibilities.

The German philosopher, Friedrich Nietzsche, wrote that a man who transcends the conventional thinking of his time "must be accustomed to living on mountain tops."

It is healthy to gaze into the distance – from a mountain top, or out over the ocean – and consider what might be.

You can reevaluate where you are when you can see a long way ahead.

Mostly, when you play, you aren't alone. You play with friends.

Humans are social animals. We require interaction with others, just as we require sleep, to survive.

Evolutionary science offers an explanation for the human instinct to seek attention and approval not only from parents, but from everyone around us.

Humans, with their gigantic brains, take a long time to reach maturity.

An orangutan reaches adolescence at age four. He is in almost unbroken skin contact with his mother for the first months and in contact nearly that close for the first few years, at which point he becomes independent.

A human doesn't reach adolescence until about thirteen. He depends on the care of others for a uniquely long time – over a decade.

No wonder a human child senses his life might depend upon summoning attention and care from others, wherever he can find them.

No wonder you want everyone to like you.

Unfortunately, not everyone will.

The best politician in the world can't win every vote. Rejection is part of life.

But your friends are your support system.

When someone's got your back, you can take a step forward.

The question for many of my patients is how to enrich their lives by making friends.

You can start by asking yourself what makes you like another person.

It's typically not a matter of talent, success or good looks. That stuff only goes so far.

More likely, you are drawn to someone who looks you in the eye, tells you his truth, and listens when you tell him yours. Someone who brings you his best self, then sustains an authentic contact, staying connected with you – actually paying attention and hearing what you say.

That's how you make a friend.

If you give someone a good listen, you're doing more than you think.

We all want a connection that's real – to be listened to and understood.

The first patient of my career was an older man who'd lost his wife of twenty-two years. He confronted me early on.

This isn't going to work.

Why is that?

You're too young. You won't understand.

I'm willing to listen.

He shrugged, unconvinced, but we got started.

He talked about his wife. After a while, he began to weep.

And weep. And weep.

It wasn't always pleasant to be in that room. I was new to the job, and I'd never witnessed grief like that. But I kept listening.

Fifteen weekly appointments passed.

At the end of the final session, he apologized for trying to fire me.

You helped. You're a pretty good therapist.

I didn't offer any solutions. But I listened, and we sustained a contact. I tolerated his feelings. He shared his truth with me, and found his own answers.

Sustaining a contact isn't easy.

Some people don't seem worth the effort.

What makes a person hard to deal with tells you something about him.

A loud, repetitious person isn't used to being heard.
Maybe, in the past, he never got a good listen.
Let him know you're there. Give him a few mm-hm's, or paraphrase something he's said back to him.
If he knows you're listening, he might show you a different side.

A boring person isn't telling the whole truth, or he'd be interesting.
Usually he's giving you what he thinks you want – and hiding anger, which he assumes you don't want.
Let him know you're okay with honesty.

A person who's unfriendly feels misunderstood.
I ask people flat out sometimes: Am I misunderstanding you?
It's important to know, and you can't mind-read. You have to ask.
The jazz saxophonist, John Coltrane, was often described as a serious man who never smiled. In reality, he was a sweetheart – just self-conscious about his crooked teeth.
You have to ask, in order to understand someone else's thoughts and feelings.

Sometimes you have to walk away if you want someone to follow.
That's how my neighbor saved his dog, Margaret.
She was a rescue. When she arrived, her coat was matted and filthy, so he took her to the groomer, who shaved her so close her collar slipped off.

Margaret ran into the traffic on Seventh Avenue.

He didn't pursue her. Instead, he took two steps back, onto the sidewalk. Margaret grew curious and followed. A bystander scooped her up and carried her to safety.

Somehow, my neighbor understood that a traumatized animal would run away if pursued. She expected to be chased.

A person who doesn't want to hear you probably needs the message delivered in a different way.

Telling the truth is vital to friendship, but the truth can hurt.

A technique called the "I-statement" or "leading with your feelings" is designed for conveying difficult truths.

It's simple. You talk about how you are feeling. Then you link your feelings to events.

An example:

A friend cancels dinner. You're angry. Hurt. Worried your friend doesn't care.

Old predictions well up. Your parents used to cancel on you like that. They never cared.

Push that aside. Stay present. Address your friend, not your past.

Don't tell him how he feels.

You didn't even stop to consider my feelings.

That's mind-reading. You don't know that.

Don't attack him, either.

You are an inconsiderate friend.

Attacks only hurt people, and raise defenses.

Maintain the contact, and report your feelings. Do not try to explain his.

The focus is you. Your feelings. That's all you know for sure.

Formulate an I-statement, leading with your feelings:
I felt hurt, and scared, and a little bit angry...
Then link those feelings to events:
...when you cancelled dinner the other night.

An I-statement has the best chance, of any spoken statement, at getting through and being heard. That's because it isn't threatening. You explain yourself to your friend, not the other way around.

That's also why an I-statement is tough to deliver. It forces you to stay conscious and be your best self.

It's easier to complain or attack, or storm off. Harder to admit someone hurt your feelings.

It takes strength to show weakness.

Getting an I-statement out can feel like a physical effort.

I once asked an older therapist colleague whether he thought it was possible for me to psychoanalyze myself along the lines of Freud's famous self-analysis. By applying the theoretical matrix of psychoanalysis to my own experience, I thought I might gain awareness and live more consciously.

You could pull it off, he admitted. But there wouldn't be much point.

We need one another to heal and grow.

Venture into the world. Play well with others.
It is a path to joy.

WORKING

A Voyage of Discovery

Instead of viewing a job as a task, consider it is a role. Not a thing, but a person.

If you are unhappy at your job, it might be that you can do the work, but the job doesn't reflect your authentic self.

It would be nice to know your calling early on, like Mozart, who composed sonatas when he was five. That's not typical.

As a teenager, your career dreams collide with reality when you discover your talents and aptitudes are limited by nature, not choice.

You have all the commitment it takes to be a rock star... but none of the talent. That's a harsh, if commonplace realization.

You tend – especially as an adolescent – to imagine yourself as the protagonist in a heroic narrative. It can be crushing to realize you are limited by banal realities.

Too short to be a basketball star.

Too out-of-tune to be the next Beyoncé.

Once you learn this lesson, you catch your breath, and

change course – you'll just find something you're good at, and do it. That's when you hit a second realization.

Even if you have the talent and aptitude for a certain job – you also have to "be" that job. It has to represent who you are.

You have to know who you are before you can know what you want to do.

Think about work, and how it came into being.

Humans were originally hunter-gatherers.

The break-down of labor must have been simple. Men went hunting in the bush. Women took care of the kids and whatever tasks could be handled close to the settlement.

With the arrival of agriculture and domesticated livestock – and higher population – specialization arrived.

The Middle Ages in Europe saw the rise of guilds – early unions for skilled laborers.

There was also more leisure time – at least for the wealthy classes – so artists and musicians began to appear. A king or a duke might hire you to set gemstones on snuff boxes, so he could hand them out as keepsakes.

You can view this development in one of two ways:

There was a need for lavish snuffboxes and someone had to be found to make them. Or there was someone out there with the idea and the inclination to make lavish snuffboxes, and he found an opportunity to follow his dream.

The second explanation makes more sense.

As societal roles became specialized, people were able to express who they were by finding a niche where they fit in.

Each "job" or "career" represents some person finding an outlet to express himself.

It isn't about finding something you can do.

It's about discovering who are you, the job that reflects your identity.

Finding your work takes time. The task might feel overwhelming, but cannot be avoided.

Money can be a distraction. As a general principle, if you put money before people – including yourself – it will always end badly.

If you love your work, the money takes care of itself. And it's worth a lot to wake up in the morning looking forward to your day.

In psychotherapy, money is often a surrogate for security in love.

If you felt insecure in your parents' care as a child, you will probably worry about money.

If you felt loved and appreciated as a kid, you're probably not unduly concerned about finances.

Either way, money won't make you live forever.

Steve Ross, the Time/Life magnate, earned seventy-eight million dollars in 1990.

He died of prostate cancer in 1992.

I treated a couple who complained all the time about money. They had a nice house, beautiful children, everything they needed – but money was the focus of conversation.

His father died when he was young, leaving the family destitute, so he grew up feeling abandoned and insecure.

Her older brother used her college tuition money to go to medical school. She grew up feeling deprived and resentful.

When this couple complained about money, they were communicating old traumas – the loss of a father, a daughter's rejection.

They had everything they needed but the sense of security that comes with growing up loved.

The craving for security can also surface in compulsive shopping or collecting.

One of my patients collected comic books. He didn't read most of them. But he always bought the complete set, then packed them away.

It wasn't about comics. It was about safety. He needed the complete set to feel secure.

How would he feel if a fire destroyed his entire collection?

He answered quickly:

Profound relief.

A boring job doesn't create stability, either. It wastes time. You can spend years hiding in a cube farm, only to be laid off on an hour's notice.

Change is always coming, and it will find you. That might be for the best.

A job should express who you are.

But it doesn't have to define you.

One of my patients told me she wasn't an interesting person because she hadn't "accomplished anything."

I reminded her she hadn't yet found what she wanted to do. She was lost at that point in time – doing the hard work of finding herself so she could "accomplish something."

"Does it have to take so long?" She asked.

Sometimes it does. Beating yourself up will only make you anxious, which will make it harder to concentrate on the task at hand – relaxing and discovering who you are, and what you enjoy.

That stubborn cocktail party question is a constant source of anxiety:
So what do you do?
You might not have an answer to the real question:
Who are you?
Finding your career is a voyage into the unknown. The whole point is to get lost. That's why they call those guys in the pith helmets "explorers." They get lost in order to find their way somewhere new – and they're rightly admired for their courage.

Humiliation can have its uses, too.
Failing at something can force you to ask yourself who you are – and how your work affects your self-image.
There is a Buddhist story about humiliation.
A monk named Small Path follows the Buddha, but doesn't display much talent for his calling.
He struggles with studies, and can't seem to learn the sutras.
The Buddha takes Small Path aside and tells him not to bother coming to lessons anymore. He can remain outside the temple, and clean the other students' shoes.
Small Path obeys the Buddha's request, and sits outside cleaning while the others study.
He was the first of the Buddha's students to attain enlightenment.

It turns out it wasn't about learning sutras, or being a genius.

It was about finding his work.

The Buddha humiliated Small Path. In the process, he taught him something about himself.

Small Path wasn't the person he thought he had to be. He wasn't much good at memorizing sutras.

But he was still Small Path – unique in his own way. Cleaning shoes, he could concentrate on discovering his authentic self.

That proved more fruitful, in the long run, than trying to be someone he wasn't.

You might feel like Small Path sometimes.

Things that come easily to others might not come easily to you.

Maybe you're not doing so well at your current job.

Maybe you don't earn as much as other people you know.

But there are thoughts flickering through your mind.

You might sit somewhere, reading a book. Being yourself.

Ideas itch at you. Dreams of what you might do someday. Who you might be.

Through your work, you express your authentic self.

It is a pathway to joy.

LOVING

A Companion for the Path Forward

Most patients come to my office to talk about loving. That's their priority. They want to find love because they think it will bring them happiness.

A partnership might contribute to your happiness.

But it isn't a partner's job to make you happy.

That's a fantasy, the product of a regression back to childhood.

A partner cannot arrive like the cavalry, and come to your rescue. His role is not to help you escape from your own life.

A partner is just that – a partner. He is an ally. Together, you pursue a mutual goal.

There's a corny religious tchotchke I found hanging in someone's kitchen years ago, called "Footsteps." It sums up this syndrome.

You've probably seen it on a poster or a greeting card.

The text begins with someone complaining to God that he walked alone through the snow, because God had abandoned him.

God explains that there was only one set of footsteps in the snow because "that's when I was carrying you, my child."

It's hard to read "Footsteps" and not feel a pang.

You want to be a child again (that's the collapse fantasy) – and you want to get carried. It's nice to think you can fall and someone will be there to catch you.

But a partner is not God, or a parent or a rescuer. He's another person. A friend. A lover. Most importantly, he's an equal.

In a healthy relationship, no one is carrying anyone, no one is leaning on anyone. You're simply walking, hand in hand, toward a dream, savoring time together as you make your way forward.

One patient told me she couldn't get over a guy she'd been seeing.

He was no good for her. He didn't even seem to want to go out with her. Yet she couldn't let go.

"But I love him," she explained.

Well, in a manner of speaking. She was loving him like a child – the way a child loves a parent.

A child's love is based upon dependency. A child loves whoever takes care of him, because he cannot take care of himself.

When a young child says "I love you," he means "I worship you and you are all-powerful and I depend upon you utterly and you are everything and I couldn't survive without you."

It's the same way religious people relate to their chosen god-objects. It's no coincidence they often kneel before statues or altars and refer to "Lord" and "Almighty" and "Heavenly Father," and so on.

If you live on an island with a volcano and it erupts and burns down your village, you can respond as an adult, and take up volcanology research. Or you can regress under stress into a child, and talk to the volcano as a parent-object, asking what you did wrong to make it angry, and trying to please it.

A child is so utterly dependent upon a parent that, if he displeases the parent, he will always locate the fault within. He will not think – oh, it's just a volcano, they erupt sometimes. It must be about the child, something he did – his fault.

My client was relating to the guy she was dating the same way. And she was beating herself up pretty bad.

Adult love is different from child love. It begins with loving yourself.

Then you add three ingredients:

Attraction, Trust, and Respect.

That's what it means to love someone else, romantically, as an adult.

Attraction. This is simple enough – you must be attracted to your partner.

You cannot go out with the guy you should go out with. You have to go out with the guy you want to go out with.

"He's so nice" is not a reason to date someone. You have to be into him, too.

Sex has a pragmatic aspect. There's room for compromise, but tastes tend to be hard-wired, and the end result has to make you happy.

Either you can live with dressing up in that Little Bo Peep costume, or you can't.

Trust. If someone values you, his attention is focused on you.

Monogamy is the clearest manifestation of a mutual fascination. If you are not being monogamous, you are looking for someone else.

Even at the start, trust can be an issue.

Are you wondering whether he'll call?

If he values you, he won't leave you wondering.

Another lovely person is always coming around the corner – that never changes.

And there is nothing wrong with being single. The freedom can be exhilarating.

But being single and in a relationship at the same time is impossible.

It's a trade-off.

If you want to be single, break up. Don't cheat, or pretend to be in an "open relationship."

A sexual friendship is not a relationship. The element of trust is missing.

That comes with monogamy.

The downside of being single is that it never builds into anything more. As you switch from person to person, you are still alone.

You have your friends, and your work, and the freedom to go out and date.

But you are missing the third element of life – loving.

After any sexual contact, there is a moment of awkwardness – two people have come close physically and emotionally.

You can run from it, but there it is.

After sex with a stranger, there's an urge to escape – to mumble excuses, flee the scene and be by yourself.

Sex with your partner entails doing something primal and intimate with your closest friend. You can't hide.

Sex is a barometer of communication in a relationship – a measure of trust.

If you aren't having sex with one another, you probably aren't telling one another the full truth about your thoughts and feelings.

Respect. Respect means an "as-is" purchase.

You accept your partner the way he is.

You cannot change him. You shouldn't want to.

He shouldn't want to change you.

Successful relationships are based in mutual admiration – and a touch of mystery.

No one knows what Napoleon saw in Josephine, Gertrude saw in Alice B, or John saw in Yoko.

Attraction, trust and respect create balance in a relationship.

Without that equilibrium, one partner becomes problematized, and the other over-performs to compensate.

That pattern of imbalance is at the root of all relationship dysfunction.

One of my patients came to me recently looking like he'd been through a war.

He plopped down in a chair and began to weep, and it didn't take long to realize he'd been "dumped." At least, that's how he characterized it.

But getting "dumped" doesn't exist. Here's why:

A partnership is a system of two. Nothing is unilateral in a partnership. If your partner "dumped" you, and you're surprised, that means you've been ignoring signals and your partner has been colluding with you in not presenting his honest feelings.

You've been "problematized" – you're too delicate to hear the truth.

He's over-performing to compensate – tip-toeing around and not telling you how he really feels.

You've joined in a conspiracy to avoid facing reality.

This is where balance comes in – the balance that comes from two whole people – not two half-people – coming together to share a walk down the path of life.

To achieve balance, you must learn to love yourself, to make yourself whole.

A child looks to his parent to tell him he is good and worthy of love.

An adult is different – you are self-sufficient. You can tell it to yourself.

You wear a price tag around your neck – and you assign the price.

That price tag shouldn't say "best offer accepted."

It should say "one million dollars."

Otherwise you are selling yourself too cheap to someone who doesn't deserve you.

You need to love yourself in order to parent yourself.

You need to parent yourself to separate from the child and become an adult.

Then you can join forces with another adult.

An equal partner cannot "dump" another equal partner.

That would violate the laws of physics.

The two primary patterns of dysfunction in a relationship are infatuation and codependence.

They begin, like all relationship problems, with imbalance – you regress into a child, and relate to your partner as a parent instead of an equal.

With infatuation, you relate to your partner like a child looking to a parent for affirmation.

In co-dependence, you relate to your partner like a child offering care to a parent because he is afraid to ask for care for himself.

Infatuation

Infatuation begins with low self-esteem, and the desire to replace your identity with somebody else's. In response to not loving yourself, you seek to disappear into an idealized partner who doesn't return your interest.

The result is a lot of unnecessary pain.

When you first experiment with romance, you are little more than a child, so it feels natural to regress into idealizing your partner the way a child idealizes a parent.

But everyone, including you, wants a self-assured, confident adult for a partner, not a clinging child.

Human beings are drawn to those who care for and celebrate themselves. Once you've proven you can go it alone, everyone else shows up to help.

I read an interview with a rap star who said he couldn't appear at a restaurant nowadays without people asking what they could do for him.

He'd just stepped out of a Maybach limousine, he said. He didn't need any help.

Years ago, when he was a drug addict living on the street, he could have used it.

Back then, people saw a hopeless case and avoided him. They could sense he wasn't taking care of himself.

It might seem unfair, but that's how things work.

A model of infatuation:

You are a shy young woman. You meet an older, charismatic man.

Your shyness is crippling. You find yourself clamming up around other people – you can barely get two words out. He, on the other hand, is the life of the party.

You can't imagine that someone so perfect – everything you wish you were – could ever be interested in you.

To your surprise, he asks you out on a date.

You're walking on air. You imagine becoming this man's wife. You'd share his life, and receive the attention and respect he attracts wherever he goes. You could finally do it – escape from your old, shy self into another, better life.

Then things fall apart.

The first date doesn't go well.

You're awestruck and clam up, and he seems impatient.

After a couple more dates, he stops calling.

Your dreams come crashing down, and you feel more trapped than ever in your terrible, hateful self. Life feels unbearable.

You cannot stop tormenting yourself with the thought that you blew it – you drove him away. It's all your fault. You hate yourself. You hate being you.

Patients show up at my office all the time recounting this sort of experience.

I do my best to explain what happened, so it doesn't happen again.

Infatuation begins with the selection of a seductive rejecting love object: you chase someone who is less interested in you than you are in him.

On the face of it, this seems illogical, and raises the question: why would you want to go out with someone who doesn't want to go out with you?

The answer is that you cannot respect someone who values you if you do not value yourself. If you write "one dollar" on your price tag – and that's what you truly feel you're worth – you aren't going to respect someone who offers you a million. You'd rather chase a person who knows how worthless you are – then try to trick him into making the purchase.

As Groucho Marx put it – you wouldn't want to join a club that would have you as a member.

The same pattern we saw with depression begins to take hold.

The child experiences rejection, locates the fault within, and struggles to delight the rejecting parent-object, as though his life depended on it.

That's why infatuation hurts so much – you re-live parental rejection, the terrible certainty that the problem is within you, not the other person.

You also feel – just as you did as a child relating to your parent – that your life depends on another person's approval.

Your first priority, in the throes of infatuation, is to cure whatever it is that renders you un-lovable.

That's where the fantasy of merger begins.

If you could make a parent-substitute love you, you could escape from being yourself and disappear into someone else – someone better.

Someone who corrects everything broken in you.

This fantasy of merging with the love-object, and being corrected by that merger, is what makes infatuation so intoxicating.

The rejecting love object becomes a symbolic antidote to whatever is wrong inside you, and you live a fantasy of escaping from who you are into the life of that love-object.

You might even fantasize about inhabiting the love-object's body, living in his home, having his life.

In the early stages of an infatuation, when the merger still seems possible, you feel you are walking on air, living at one hundred percent.

The stars shine brighter.

The air tastes better.

The highs are higher.

You are LIVING.

This is what all those songs about being in love are about.

If only it could last.

But the merger you long for amounts to self-annihilation.

You are not only gratified by escaping into a new identity – you are also sadistically gratified by killing yourself off.

The Stockholm Syndrome is a phenomenon in which hostages held for a long period begin siding with their abductors.

It applies perfectly to the scenario of an infatuation – you give yourself over to the enemy.

Someone rejects you – the seductive rejecting love-object – and you join them in that rejection, then take it to a new level, plotting your own annihilation.

You resemble the child who asks to be returned to an abusive home.

Like that child, you chase a rejecting love-object because you locate the fault within – and dread being left alone with your faulty, broken self. Like that child, you are willing to participate in your own destruction in order to escape into the merger with a love-object who doesn't want you.

Like many victims of oppression, you end up hating yourself more than your tormentors ever could.

That's why the the worst misogynists are women, the worst racists members of the oppressed race, and the worst homophobes homosexuals.

They long for acceptance, but find only rejection. Like children desperate for love, they blame themselves, and join their oppressors.

That's how the military turns adolescents into soldiers.

They send a young person to a stressful environment – like basic training – which regresses him.

They present a seductive-rejecting love object – a drill sergeant.

Initially, this idealized parent-object does nothing but heap abuse on the new recruit, letting him know he is not living up to expectations.

Eventually the tough-as-nails sergeant begins to offer a trickle of grudging acceptance.

Before long, the recruit is under his spell – he begins to achieve "unit cohesion."

Infatuated by a seductive, rejecting love object, he'd do almost anything to please.

This comes in very useful during a war.

At some point in a full-blown infatuation, your self-esteem feels entirely dependent upon the love object's feedback.

Like a child seeking to please a parent, you study every gesture, every hint of how the object might feel about you, and make his reaction the basis for your self-esteem.

But the love-object doesn't care about you – he's probably indifferent, or a little annoyed.

Thus your celebration of the love-object becomes inversely proportional to your image of yourself.

He's so great...I'm so worthless.

He's so handsome...I'm so ugly.

He's so interesting...I'm so boring.

On and on.

Eventually, the indifference of the rejecting love-object becomes a club you use to to bash yourself over the head.

At some level, it feels good.

It is an outlet for aggression against the child, whom you seek to kill off. Discharging aggression is inherently gratifying – even aggression turned in upon the self.

At this point, your sole obsession is the merger – the craving to escape into the other.

Needless to say – infatuation hurts. It is painful to feel that you need someone else's love in order to love yourself – especially if you know that other person's love is not forthcoming.

If this happens to you, here's what to do:

First: Remember this is about you, not the love-object.

This entire process, including the pain, originates from you and is about you and no one else.

Stop obsessing about the other person.

You shouldn't call him again.

It doesn't matter whether he might have accidentally erased your email and not read it.

It doesn't matter whether that ever-so-slightly ambiguous comment he made three weeks ago when you ran into him on the sidewalk might have meant more than it seemed.

This is not about the other person.

It's about you.

An infatuation will never work because it is out of balance and therefore not a true partnership.

You cannot escape into someone else. You must love yourself before you can expect anyone else to love you.

Second: Get in touch with your anger.

Infatuation reproduces the conditions which, when present in childhood, result in depression – forbidden anger at an idealized object.

You are trying to please an ideal, parent-like object, whom you feel you are too dependent upon to get angry at, even when he rejects you.

This situation isolates you from your right to anger and tears down your self-esteem.

Treat infatuation like depression. Give yourself the right to be angry.

Don't go into action on the anger – own your right to hear it and understand it.

Getting rejected is annoying, especially by someone you admire.

He has a right to reject you.

And you have a right to your anger.

Anger isn't rational or logical – it just is.

The object of your infatuation is a person, with his own issues. At some level, he might enjoy your worship. Being admired is a guilty pleasure. Maybe he did tease you or flirt with you, or simply enjoy the attention.

If you feel you were toyed with, or given mixed messages, maybe you were.

Either way, your feelings are real.

He's just a person – and you have a right to own your anger.

Your best self is still there, within you.

You've been rejected, but one person's response to you – which might have nothing to do with who you are – isn't a referendum on your value as a human being.

Remember who you were before all this drama.

You had hobbies, opinions, friends, a job. Playing. Working.

Go back to a "you" place. Spend time with yourself.

You needn't experience solitude as abandonment.

It might have felt that way when you were a child, but you are an adult now.

You aren't abandoned – you cannot be abandoned. You have yourself for company – and you have your friends.

Spend time doing things you enjoy, with people you enjoy, at places you enjoy.

When your self-esteem needs a boost, it might be time to disappear into your own uniqueness.

Snuggle in bed with a little dog.

Listen to scratchy old jazz recordings.

Read long books on Chinese history.

Make a big pot of split pea soup.

Do what makes you happy. Be good to yourself. You deserve care and love.

Sometimes remembering your quirky side reminds you that you're human.You have uniqueness and value like everyone else.

Make authentic contact with yourself.

Drop preconceptions of who you are, stay in the moment, and listen to your heart.

This is like re-parenting. It involves being there for yourself, in a caring way. Listening to your own voice.

There's a person inside you. A person you may come to respect.

You don't need talent or fame or beauty.

They're nice, but you can live without them.

You can be a person you respect just for facing the world each day as your best self, without apology, and connecting honestly with other people.

Human beings are capable of enormous change.

You decide who to be each day. There's no reason to reject yourself.

You can love who you are because you control who you are.

You can learn to love the child who lives on within you.

All things must pass – even heartbreak.

Impossible as it might seem, if you find your way back to loving yourself, the spell of infatuation will lift.

Then you can work on the underlying issue – an unhappiness with who you are, dating back to messages you received as a child.

Codependence

At first glance, codependence, like infatuation, appears bizarre.

You take care of another person – someone you might not even like – in order to communicate your own need for care.

My patient, Alice, was in a codependent relationship for twelve years.

Alice met her partner right after they graduated from college.

From the start, she was supporting them both. Her partner never took a job, always providing lame excuses, then angry outbursts to keep the subject from being discussed.

Before long, the partner was having sex outside the relationship, and treating Alice with condescension and abuse.

Alice's friends faded away. They couldn't stand her partner, and were frustrated by the situation.

Alice stayed in this codependent relationship for more than a decade because caring for this person was the only way she could find to communicate her needs.

It took months of work before Alice could admit she hated her free-loading partner, own her anger at her, and take steps to reclaim her life, bringing herself the care she needed instead of lavishing it on someone undeserving.

Codependence is remarkably stubborn, but it can be overcome.

The pattern of codependence begins in homes where children are not permitted to put words to their needs.

Maybe your parents are distracted by their own struggles, or overwhelmed by the task of parenting. Either way, the message is clear: Don't bother us with your problems.

You are forced to turn to other means to signal that you have needs.

The most acceptable method is doing for others what you need done for you. You become the best kid in the world – making everyone else happy.

All the while, you dream of having that care returned.

At the core of codependence, there is a phenomenon I call birthday party syndrome. Oddly enough, the codependent pattern emerges into bold relief around the topic of birthdays.

You associate birthdays with early childhood – that's when you first experienced the delight of this special day.

It is a magical event for a child. You are singled out and celebrated for being born. If you're lucky enough to have parents who put in the work, your birthday might be a dream come true. Friends appear out of the blue, bringing you gifts, lavishing attention. All you have to do is show up.

For children who don't have such marvelous birthdays, the fantasy might be even stronger. The longing grows for a magical day when everyone knows exactly what you need, and provides it – asking nothing in return.

The ultimate birthday fantasy is the surprise party.

Everyone secretly prepares a celebration of you, then jumps out to shout "Surprise!" followed by cake and friendship and gifts.

This fantasy recurs in Hollywood movies.

Think of any film with teenage or sports themes, or any biopic with a heroic subject. There's always the same scene at the end:

The hero feels discouraged after struggling with the slings and arrows of outrageous fortune.

A friend arrives, reminding him of a seemingly unimportant meeting.

The hero grudgingly agrees to attend.

He approaches a door...there's a moment's hesitation before he opens it and then...

The whole school.

The entire stadium.

Everyone in the office.

Take your pick.

They're all there to let him know how much they appreciate everything he does for them.

The scene begins with one person clapping. It catches on, and the entire room rises to its feet and the hero's face breaks into a smile, the music soars, and he's beaming, tears trickling down his face.

He was right after all.

They do love him.

The climactic scene of Mr. Holland's Opus is a good example. There are hundreds of others. Rent a few feel-good films and you'll spot them right away.

Movies are fantasies. They provide the vicarious experiences we crave.

You want one of those scenes.

You want to clutch a statuette and thank the Academy.

But how?

You aren't really expecting the entire school to meet you in the auditorium for a long-overdue standing ovation, but it would be nice if someone remembered your birthday.

You want a surprise party.

As you get older, birthdays change. There are no more parents doing the planning. You are alone. Your friends might not remember.

This make you angry, scared and hurt.

Where is everyone? Why aren't they taking care of you?

If you are able to put your feelings into words, and ask for what you need, or provide it for yourself, you're all set. Call your friends, plan the party you want – or take yourself out on your own to celebrate.

Sounds like fun.

Except birthdays trigger codependent feelings.

The first step down the path to codependence is acting-in: shutting down with your feelings of anger and hurt. You don't do anything for your birthday, just wait and see if anyone remembers. That's what surprise parties are all about – right? You wait, and they come through – or they don't.

That's acting-in.

The next step is throwing birthday parties for everyone else, so they'll know what you want.

That's the beginning of codependence.

You model what you want done for you because you don't know how to ask for it.

If you do it for them, then they have to do it for you – don't they? Especially if you go overboard, and give them everything they could want. That way, they have to do it for you.

Except they don't.

This strategy doesn't work.

Codependence doesn't work.

It's like living your life on a perpetual hunger strike – denying yourself as an act of protest. You end up starving.

People tend to take their lead not from how you treat them, but from how you treat yourself. If you ignore yourself, they will ignore you, too.

Codependence makes for disappointing birthdays. It also makes for disastrous relationships. Codependent partnerships can drag on for decades.

The pattern becomes self-perpetuating because you continue doubling down, raising the stakes as you give and give and never get anything in return for your investment.

A martyr element comes into play as well. You will sacrifice for him until you die, and then he will regret never appreciating you.

But victory through defeat amounts to defeat.

You end up angry, hurt and sad.

And the partner who exploits a codependent has his own issues. The care-taking relationship infantilizes him, regressing him into a helpless child.

Relationships go out of balance, and create dysfunctional patterns like infatuation and codependence for a simple reason: If you don't love yourself, and learn to care for yourself, you are in no position to enter a partnership.

It's like the oxygen mask on an airplane. Put it on yourself first or you can't be there for anyone else.

Making a Partnership Work for You

We've defined a healthy relationship, and talked about how things can go wrong. Now it's time to address the practical issue of finding a partner – someone who might be right for you.

The process is a bit like a business transaction – to complete the exchange, you have to be sure of what you're selling and what you're buying.

What you're selling is you.

If you're wearing a million dollar price tag, people will sit up and take notice.

But you have to believe you're worth what you're charging.

Sometimes I ask my patients to guess the value of the artworks hanging in my office.The pieces are mostly by friends and acquaintances.

Some people like the big abstract pastel with blue and pink scribbles. It was a gift. Supposedly, it's worth a couple thousand dollars.

My favorite is an etching of two men sitting at a cafe table in Paris – maybe because it's by my great-uncle. I don't know what it's worth, but it's my partner's favorite, too. He's an amateur portrait painter, and admires the expressiveness of the faces.

One of my patients always found that particular piece distracting. The man sitting on the right side of the cafe table looked exactly like her father. She preferred to sit in a chair facing away from that etching – it got on her nerves.

Everyone responds to a different piece of art for a different reason, and no one really knows what any work of art is worth because it's worth something different to each person.

You're like a work of art. You are unique, and your value is dependent upon your own appraisal.

Be a masterpiece. Locate a connoisseur.

Don't sell your Rembrandt at a garage sale.

Don't de-value yourself because of the way you look, either.

Everyone has some aspect of their appearance they'd like to change. One of my patients, Tom, explained to me in detail why he was ugly and no one could possibly find him attractive.

This was news to me, because so far as I could tell Tom was a handsome guy – film star handsome. It was a puzzling case.

Tom had been told by various people that he was handsome, and some had even attempted to pursue him, but he'd always dismissed their interest. He couldn't accept that other people didn't see what he saw when he looked in the mirror: he was too short, had bad skin, bad teeth, a bump on his nose.

Even as he enumerated these terrible flaws, I strained to see what he was talking about. I looked – and saw a handsome guy.

The problem wasn't with how Tom looked. It was with the messages he was given as a child.

Tom's parents had him when they were very young, and their marriage soon broke up. The father, caught up in a nasty divorce battle, fought for custody of his son and won it, only to dump the boy on resentful relatives. Tom grew up receiving the message that his presence was a nuisance – that people wished he wasn't there. He learned that he was nothing special – certainly no one whom anyone would notice or be attracted to.

Tom went on to succeed in his career, against the odds. Despite his parents' disinterest, he worked hard in school and rose to an impressive position in the business world. But he still felt ugly – nothing special. His physical appearance became a container for all the feelings his parents put in him about himself.

In our session, I reminded Tom that his parents were old now, and far away – he hardly saw them anymore. Nowadays he was the one in charge of parenting the little boy inside him. And he was doing a lousy job of it.

I asked him when he first became ugly.

He shrugged.

I asked whether he was ugly back when he was a little boy. Was he ugly at six? At ten? At twelve? When did the ugliness first arrive?

Tom shrugged again, and said he'd always felt that way.

I asked him if there was such a thing as an ugly little boy.

He said, no, probably not.

So were you ugly when you were seven?

He said he didn't know – probably.

I said of course not. There is no such thing as an ugly seven-year-old. In fact there is no such thing as an ugly child. No child is ugly because every child is unique and beautiful.

So why are you treating this child with such cruelty – telling him such terrible things about who he is?

The messages Tom was addressing to his child were the same ones his parents sent him, voices that were put inside him as a child, messages that kept playing years later, like:

You are a nuisance. You are nothing special. You are always in the way. We wish you weren't here.

I asked him to create some healthier messages for his child self.

He looked at me blankly. Like what?

Well, let's pretend your mother wasn't absent from your life when you were little. Let's pretend she took you up in her lap when you were a boy and said something like:

You are my little one, my precious little fellow. You are handsome and good and you make me proud. You are my boy, my special boy. You are beautiful. You are my treasure.

Tears started to run down Tom's face.

She never said anything like that.

I know. But you can say it. You don't have to feel ugly. There's nothing ugly in you and nothing ugly about you. You deserve love because you are beautiful. Inside and out.

Please don't tell your child he is ugly. He isn't. He's you, and he deserves your love, so he can learn to accept love from the world outside. It's critical to his happiness. Please be a better parent to that little child.

Now for what you're buying.

A partner is a best friend.

The same rules that apply to meeting a best friend apply to meeting a partner.

You wouldn't expect to acquire a best friend right away. It takes time to pick the right person, develop a connection and share experiences.

It isn't always who you meet, either. Sometimes it's when you meet him.

You both have to be ready. It has to be the right time.

Patients complain there are no good men out there. Or no good women. Or no one their age. Or no one interesting.

But there are.

You're looking for a needle in a haystack – but you only need one needle.

If you go out into the world expecting to meet good people, they're out there. But you have to get out and look.

It's like electrons – you need a lot of motion to get a collision.

Relationships are organic, too – like leaves. You can't pull on a leaf to make it longer – it has to grow at its own pace, in its own direction.

If things don't work out, it doesn't mean anyone's failed.

Some relationships are brief, but meaningful.

Others run on for years, more from momentum than inspiration.

You may have several meaningful relationships during your life, important at different times, for different reasons.

Above all else, a relationship should be fun.

I'm not being flippant. A relationship should be a pathway to joy.

The best measure of success in a relationship is simple: how much of the time you're having fun being together.

You'll never get one hundred percent good times, but if you're under fifty percent, something's wrong.

There is nothing sacred about a relationship.

Human history will proceed whether or not you stay with your partner.

If it feels like the Earth will cease to spin unless you're together with someone else, there is a problem.

That sounds more like a child terrified of abandonment than an adult choosing a partner.

You can handle a break-up.

Couples arrive at my office seeking permission to call it quits.

They already have permission.

Don't stay in a relationship for other people.

No one is surprised when you break up.

They are amazed when you stay together.

And it's none of their business.

Don't stay in a relationship because it's nice to have a warm body on the other side of the bed.

A partner is not a teddy bear.

Don't stay in a relationship because you're married.

Marriage has sentimental appeal.

But ceremonies and legal niceties are not the basis for a partnership.

You can't promise your partner eternal love.

No one can make that promise.

Don't stay in a relationship for your kids.

Divorce doesn't hurt children. Living in an unhappy situation hurts children.

Don't stay in a relationship if you rarely see one another.

A long-distance relationship is like being single without the fun.

Don't stay in a relationship if your partner wants to break up.

If you are ignoring signals, you are colluding in a lie.

A few words about happy relationships.

According to Tolstoy, "Happy families are all alike; every unhappy family is unhappy in its own way."

All happy couples are alike in one respect: There isn't much drama.

If you're arguing about everything and it starts to feel like the Israelis and the Palestinians – it might be time for something new.

A relationship shouldn't be a constant struggle.

There's an old saying that you can't write a novel about a happy couple because there'd be nothing to write about.

Happy couples are so quiet they're easy to miss.

I don't believe people who say they're not looking for a relationship.

It's human nature to couple. You're looking unless you're in one.

You need to play. You need to work. You need to love.

Not looking for a relationship means something else.

I'm not attracted to you, or I'm scared and want to go slow.

Or I don't feel ready because first I need to love myself.

But everyone is looking.

Loving is the final challenge.

Share your life with a partner. Walk a path together, hand in hand.

It may bring you joy.

A Final Note on Raising a Child

———— ✦ ————

The decision to raise a child deserves a separate book.

I've taken a middle path – adding a few observations.

I've separated this discussion from the chapter on loving because raising a child extends beyond your relationship with your partner. It involves a new person, and a new relationship.

If you decide to bring a child into your life, you complete a circle, assuming the role your parent played for you.

It's your turn to do the impossible job.

Your child will always relate to you, at some level, as the person you are when you raise him. Your behavior will affect the way he relates to the world.

That's a tremendous responsibility.

You, and your life, may affect him in ways that are unfathomable to you.

Raising a child isn't for everyone.

Few parents express regret over having a child, but no study shows that raising children increases happiness.

Two things are certain:

Raising a child may or may not add meaning to your life.

No one is required to bring another human being into the world.

People offer selfless reasons for raising a child, but there are unconscious feelings at play. At some level, you have a child because you want to. You do it to please yourself.

Here are some reasons patients have given me for raising a child, along with a brief response:

I want to give a child everything I never had.

This appears selfless, but a danger exists in over-identifying with the child. You could end up raising yourself for a second time instead of raising him.

If you grew up poor, it feels good to provide your child with material things – but children don't need that. You may be addressing your issues, not his.

You might also try to lavish love on your child that you never received.

That might overwhelm him.

If you want to do better for your child than your parents did for you, start by raising him for who he is – not who you were.

A child has a unique voice and unique needs. Just like you.

He cannot re-live your childhood.

I want to mold and shape a little life and teach it right from wrong.

Children are not clay. They seem like it when they're young because they learn through imitation. But they will rebel and surprise you – just as you surprised your parents.

You can debate nature versus nurture, but genes are important. They hold sway over much of a person's personality, preferences and predispositions. So do the influences of peers and community.

Your mother and father probably thought they could mold you and teach you to share their views and beliefs. It didn't work. You turned out differently from them.

Your child will be different from you. That is his right.

He might not agree with your taste in music or your politics.

You can't change him.

The things you tell your child are less important than listening and sustaining a connection.

Hearing I love you means less to a child than hearing I like you and believing it.

I want someone who will totally and entirely love me.

A twenty-two year old mother told me this. She had her first child at sixteen. Now she wanted another.

Her logic was backwards. A child shouldn't love you. You should love him.

He may love you, but that is his choice.

Don't enter into parenthood to become a child who demands love.

That young mother was still in high school. The father was absent. The grandmother did most of the parenting.

The son may love his mother. He may also grow to resent her absence from his early life. He has a right to those feelings.

I want someone to take care of me in my old age.

It is a noble thing to care for your elders.

A friend of mind is Chinese, and he follows his cultural tradition by financially supporting his parents. He has done so since his first job bagging groceries in junior high school.

Twenty years later, he hands them part of his paycheck each month. I know he has mixed feelings about it.

He is grateful to his parents for bringing him to the United States from China and providing him with opportunity.

He is frustrated his siblings don't share more of the burden.

He resents his parents' demands for more and their squirreling away of money he feels they don't need.

It is a sensitive subject.

The impulse to care for another person should come from the heart – not from guilt or a sense of duty. Removing the element of personal choice creates resentment.

I want a big house full of children.

Huge "broods" of children aren't as much fun as they seem in the movies.

In the Hollywood version, a house "bursting" with children is invariably hilarious and charming.

In real life, large families can be happy – but there are challenges.

There is less money. Plenty of love might help, but kids cope with less. Their classmates get toys, vacations, clothes, dinners out, trips to the movies. They don't.

More importantly, space can be tight. Children share bedrooms. Privacy is sacrificed. That's hard on teenagers.

Time is rationed, too. By necessity, older siblings change diapers, deal with laundry, break up arguments. Many eventually choose not to have kids of their own – they've done it already.

With little time available for each child, they receive labels:

The smart one. The popular one. The helpful one. The sporty one.

There's no time for complexity. Kids feel interchangeable.

A distracted parent can miss signs of abuse.

One of my patients suffered sexual abuse from his older brother. The mother, struggling to get by with little money in a house crowded with ten children, missed the signs. The abuse persisted for years.

As a therapist, I hear about problems with people's childhoods. Perhaps I carry a bias.

On the other hand, so does Hollywood.

I want to adopt a child who needs a home.

Adopting a child is different from having a child of your own.

You cannot remove an infant from its birth mother without negative effects. Under terrible circumstances, his parents did the unthinkable and gave him up.

He will always feel that trauma. He will long for them all his life.

There must not be any secrets around adoption. Secrets imply shame.

No one has a right to erase a person's past.

That erases his dignity.

Adopted children are traumatized children.

They are not special because they were chosen. That's a fairy tale.

They are special because their parents abandoned them.

If you choose to adopt, you probably wish to help a child in need.

Or maybe you cannot have a child of your own.

An adopted child has no choice.

He may be hyper-compliant, because he cannot afford to lose what he has.

He may test your love, afraid to trust it.

I have grown to admire many adopted people, and the parents who raised them. No one pretended it was easy.

I like kids.

This is the best reason to raise a child.

Kids are expensive and messy and frustrating, but some people revel in raising them. If you enjoyed your own childhood, and remain in close touch with your child-self, then you might, too.

Keep in mind, you don't have to raise a child to enjoy kids.

I know a therapist who does wonderful professional work with children. He's a big kid himself and fondly remembers his early childhood.

His partner doesn't care much for children – she'd rather read a book or go to the opera.

My colleague expresses his love for children through his work, and by spoiling his teenage godson, taking him for pizza and bowling while his partner stays home.

This man knows the secret of successful parents and everyone who loves children: There is no rule for relating to kids, because every child is unique, just like every adult.

My colleague happens to get along with his godson, and they click.

If you're lucky, you will click with your child. But you may have to stretch to accommodate a unique personality.

One of my patients has a nephew – a flamboyant young man at age four. His father doesn't know what to make of him. The boy doesn't care for sports, but revels in playing dress up and going shopping. Just like his uncle.

To his father's relief, they get along great.

You can only love your child as much as you love yourself.

He might look like you, sound like you and act like you. He might remind you of you. He might be different from you, and test your acceptance of difference.

He needs you to love him.

Do not take the decision to have a child lightly.

It may be a pathway to joy.

Epilogue

꧁ ꧂

This book is intended to help you get un-stuck – to instill awareness, so you can create change and locate joy.

Your world should feel comfortable, and reflect who you are.

Otherwise you're living someone else's life.

Stop doing what you are told.

That's how a child lives his life – not an adult.

Use your anger to change the world around you.

Patients tell me they can't complain. Others have it worse.

Some do. And some have it better.

You have needs like everyone else. Fulfilling those needs will bring you joy.

It may seem hopeless.

Patients say it is too late for them. They never got what they needed. Now they never will.

I tell them about resilient children.

Studies show that abused, neglected children can surprise everyone by surviving.

They manage this feat by locating surrogates. They replace what is missing or harmful in their lives with something nurturing and good – a teacher, an aunt or uncle, a neighbor down the street – someone who can provide the care they need.

Resilient kids don't let an ugly world shape who they are. They let who they are shape the world.

You can do that, too.

Even if you had it bad – very bad – as a kid, it doesn't have to mark you for life.

Some of my patients come from backgrounds marred by sexual abuse, addiction, violence, abandonment, neglect and mental illness. I have kidded a few by naming them to my "top ten list" of worst childhoods.

I also tell them what I know to be true:

You can grow up in a madhouse – practically raised by wolves – and come out just fine.

Being raised amid abuse and disorder doesn't mean you can't become your best self – exactly the person you want to be. I see it every day.

As I wrote this book, my friend, Shin, died of breast cancer.

She had two little children, Josie and Toby.

As she grew weaker and the end approached, Shin told me, again and again, that her first concern was not herself, but her husband and kids.

Before she died, Shin taught the children a game.

She would gather them to her, and look each in the eye, very seriously.

Where is mama? She asked.

And she taught them to point to their chests.

Mama's in your heart.

She held them tight.

That's where I'll always be, whenever you need me.

Shin is gone now. But Josie and Toby find her when they look inside, where her love was carefully stored away.

Resilient children.

A good parent provides you with love. You carry it within you.

Be a good parent. Never be without love.

I write about death as I write about joy.

They are inseparable.

There is a "frame" in psychotherapy, which includes an arbitrary fifty-minute time limit on a session. It's intended to create urgency.

The clock is always there, ticking away the hour.

And you will always accomplish the most during the last ten minutes.

Loss can serve as a framework for therapy.

You suffer losses in the course of a life.

And awareness always arrives with a tinge of remorse.

You wish you'd known sooner what you know now.

An old therapist I trained with used to quip:

What a fool I was at eighty, said the ninety year old man.

A final tale from Buddhism, about the Bodhisattva of Compassion.

The Bodhisattvas are followers of the Buddha who achieve sufficient wisdom to attain enlightenment, the state of nirvana.

The Bodhisattva of Compassion, alone, remains behind to assist mankind.

Three monks wander the desert until they reach a walled garden. They hear the splash of water within.

The first monk leaps into the garden and disappears.

The second, with assistance, scales the barrier and hurries away.

The third monk clambers up the wall on his own, studies the garden and listens to the water bubbling from the spring. Then he slides back down.

This is the Bodhisattva of Compassion.

His job is to search for other lost souls. He shows them how to find the garden.

This book contains lessons I learned from others, mostly my patients, as we sat together in a quiet room, doing the work of psychotherapy.

They shared their compassion and wisdom.

I have tried to put that experience into words.

The Bodhisattva of Compassion has a secret:

Enlightenment doesn't exist. Neither does nirvana.

The walled garden isn't a destination. It's a resting place.

The path to wisdom has no end.

The Bodhisattva doesn't remain behind by helping others.

He steps ahead.

Closer to joy.

ACKNOWLEDGEMENTS

I wish to thank the following individuals for offering feedback on early versions of this book, assisting in its publication or simply providing much-needed encouragement: Roz Parr, Steven Sendor, Laurel Meyerhofer, Dietrich Meyerhofer, Nancy Mitrocsak, Carol Nyikita-Moran, Bill Moran, Sydelle Kramer, Susan Rabiner, Chip Duckett, Jack Meyerhofer, Elsi Pauli, Jamie Flanders, Lars Grava, Michael Jeng, Lexy Bloom, Shin Na, Liz Nash, Danielle Sanders, Andrew Blechman, James Blechman, Tania Garcia, Lena Fugeri, Eric Kressman, Amy Kressman Brodsky, Gerald Lucas, Adam Lancaster, Zeke Dizon, Marta Pacsu, Louis Ormont, Gail Brown, Rob Wyke, Kashmir Hill, Terry LeGrand, Richard Shephard, Michael McManus, Kate Love, Tommy Cookson, Alexander Lis, Felice Picano, Joe Bain, Stephen Jay Gould, Steve Lawrence, Alejandro Madero, Mitchell Weitz, Howard Blechman, Estelle Kressman, Ricky Wai, Irene Coeny, Sandra Meyerhofer, Peter Englert, David Meyerhofer, Joan Lucas, Aurelian Lis, Jeff Conway, Judith Khan, Daniel Hilken, Viv Kee Hilken, all of my psychotherapy clients over the years and of course my partner, William Yan To Kwok. Thank you all. You had my back, so I could take a step forward.

About the Author

Will Meyerhofer, JD MSW is a psychotherapist in private practice in Lower Manhattan, in New York City. He holds degrees from Harvard College, NYU School of Law and The Hunter College School of Social Work.

CPSIA information can be obtained at www.ICGtesting.com
Printed in the USA
BVOW061045030412

286742BV00001B/117/P

9 781937 600471